D0437950

DISCARDED

Twayne's United States Authors Series

EDITOR OF THIS VOLUME

Kenneth E. Eble

University of Utah

Hamilton Basso

TUSAS 331

HAMILTON BASSO

By JOSEPH R. MILLICHAP
University of Tulsa

TWAYNE PUBLISHERS
A DIVISION OF G. K. HALL & CO., BOSTON

Published in 1979 by Twayne Publishers,
A Division of G. K. Hall & Co.
All Rights Reserved

Printed on permanent/durable acid-free paper and bound in the
United States of America

First Printing

Frontispiece photograph of Hamilton Basso by George Cserna

For Paulette

Library of Congress Cataloging in Publication Data

Millichap, Joseph R
Hamilton Basso.

(Twayne's United States authors series ; TUSAS 331)
Bibliography: p. 159–62
Includes index.
1.   Basso, Hamilton, 1904–1964
—Criticism and interpretation.
PS3503.A8423Z77   813'.5'2   79-10515
ISBN 0-8057-7225-1

Contents

About the Author

Joseph R. Millichap, a native New Yorker, studied at St. Peters College and received his Ph.D. in English from Notre Dame University. After teaching at the Universities of North Carolina, Greensboro and Montana, he came to the University of Tulsa, where is now Associate Professor of English. His special interest is American literature, particularly modern American fiction and the regional literatures of the South and West. He has published widely in these areas, as well as in the fields of general communications, film, and creative writing. His scholarship includes monographs on George Catlin and Carson McCullers, as well as a study of immigration and the American novel. During 1977-78, Dr. Millichap was Fulbright Professor of American Literature in Finland.

Preface

Hamilton Basso remains a neglected novelist of the Southern Renaissance, that sudden flowering of Southern literature which began after World War I and lasted until sometime after World War II. During this period the South lagged far behind other sections of the country in any statistical comparisons of population, wealth, or education, yet in these years it produced the Nobel Prize-winning William Faulkner, as well as Thomas Wolfe, Robert Penn Warren, Erskine Caldwell, Katherine Anne Porter, Eudora Welty, Carson McCullers, Flannery O'Connor, Caroline Gordon, Truman Capote, Peter Taylor, and William Styron in fiction; John Crowe Ransom, Allen Tate, Donald Davidson, Randall Jarrell, and James Dickey in poetry; Paul Green, Tennessee Williams, and Lillian Hellman in drama; as well as many important critics, nonfictionists, and journalists. The reasons for this explosion of talent in a region which had earlier contributed to the national literature in a much smaller way are many and complex. The most important was the conjunction of the modern movement in literature with a movement toward social and cultural reassessment in the South. Given this primary impetus, the continued interaction of talented individuals and literary groups extended the Renaissance until the 1960s, at least.

Admittedly, Hamilton Basso is not a forgotten Faulkner, but a reexamination of his fiction proves as instructive as the continual reworking of many Southern writers receiving considerable critical attention today. A lifelong friend of Faulkner's and a confidant of Wolfe's, Basso stood near the center of the Southern Renaissance from the *Double Dealer* group in New Orleans after World War I to the Northern exile of Southerners like Warren and Styron after World War II. Basso's work, as well as his life, reflects the development of the Southern Renaissance; his attempts to probe the Gothic plantation house, to picture the Southern sojourner in New York, or to portray the complex significance of a populist demagogue lend insight into the works of Faulkner, Wolfe, and Warren. At the same time Basso's fiction represents a strain different in many interesting ways from that of these novelists, the Agrarians, or the Gothicists. Basso represents the liberal and Realistic traditions of the Southern Renaissance, in contrast to the conservative, Gothic, and symbolic bent of its other fictionists. Finally, and most importantly, his fiction is interesting and rewarding in its own right; it deserves and repays continued examination and appreciation. For these reasons this study will attempt a sympathetic portrait of the man and a generous assessment of his work.

This study will follow the pattern of most Twayne volumes by presenting an overview of the author's life and work in an introductory chapter, which, in this case, will establish Hamilton Basso as a Realistic novelist of the Southern Renaissance. Succeeding chapters will analyze and interpret his novels within chronological and thematic groupings. Chapter 2 provides a careful analysis of his first novel, *Relics and Angels* (1929), which demonstrates many of the settings, characters, plots, themes, and ideas which reappear in his other books. In Chapter 3, Basso's social novels— *Cinnamon Seed* (1934), *In Their Own Image* (1935), *Courthouse Square* (1936)—are grouped together and analyzed in terms of their author's growing social commitment during the Depression. Chapter 4 groups three philosophical novels written on the eve of World War II— *Days Before Lent* (1939), *Wine of the Country* (1941), *Sun In Capricorn* (1942). Chronological sequence is sacrificed in Chapter 5, which considers Basso's two novels set outside the South— *The Greenroom* (1949) and *A Touch of the Dragon* (1964). Chapter 6 unites the two Pompey's Head novels— *The View From Pompey's Head* (1954) and *The Light Infantry Ball* (1959). Chapter 7 considers Basso's short fiction, and Chapter 8, his nonfiction. Chapter 9 provides a short conclusion which reassesses Basso's achievement in his novels.

Hopefully, this study will renew interest in Hamilton Basso's fiction, as well as contribute to the growing scholarly material on the Southern Renaissance. If it does so, I must acknowledge my general debt to the scholars who have developed the historical and bibliographical tools for continued work in this area. In the preparation of this volume I was particularly aided by the work of Professor James Rocks of Loyola University-Chicago. Mrs. Etolia Basso was also very kind in providing information not to be found in print and constructive criticism of my text. My wife, Paulette, read and discussed Basso's work with me, helping me with many insights into the novels. Margie Mainstone accurately typed my handwritten manuscript, a difficult job. The University of Tulsa provided typing, library materials, and grant support.

Acknowledgments

The following publishers have granted permission for me to quote from copyrighted compositions.

Macauley and Company for: *Relics and Angels* (1929).

Scribner and Son for: *Cinnamon Seed* (1934), *In Their Own Image* (1935), *Courthouse Square* (1936), *Days Before Lent* (1939), *Wine of the Country* (1941), *Sun In Capricorn* (1942).

Doubleday and Company for: *The Greenroom* (1949), *The View From Pompey's Head* (1954), *The Light Infantry Ball* (1959).

Viking Press for: *A Touch of the Dragon* (1964).

Chronology

1939   The Bassos live briefly in Southern France. *Days Before Lent* (novel) published.

1940   *Days Before Lent* wins Southern Authors Award; the Bassos' son, Keith, born in Asheville, North Carolina.

1941   *Wine of the Country* (novel) published; the Bassos live in Charlottesville, Virginia and South Hadley, Massachusetts.

1942   Basso goes to work for *Time* magazine; the Bassos live in New York.

1943   *Sun In Capricorn* (novel) published; the Bassos move to Weston, Connecticut.

1944   Basso working for *New Yorker,* publishing nonfiction and short stories in that magazine.

1948   Etolia Basso edits *The World From Jackson Square* (pieces on New Orleans).

1949   *The Greenroom* (novel) published.

1952   Basso edits a new edition of William Lewis Herndon's *Exploration of the Valley of the Amazon* (1842). Movie version of *Days Before Lent* (Hollywood title, *Holiday for Sinners)* made by Gerald Meyer.

1954   Basso publishes his ninth novel, *The View From Pompey's Head;* it becomes his first best-seller.

1955   Movie version of *The View From Pompey's Head* made by Phillip Dunne.

1957   Basso elected Vice-President of National Institute of Arts and Letters.

1959   *The Light Infantry Ball,* the second novel in the projected Pompey's Head trilogy, published.

1960   *A Quota of Seaweed* (travel sketches) published. Basso working on unfinished novel set in Tahiti.

1961   Basso leaves the *New Yorker;* son Keith graduates Harvard University with honors.

1962   Basso writes eulogy for Faulkner in *Saturday Review.*

1964   *A Touch of the Dragon* (novel) published. Basso dies May 13 in New Haven, Connecticut. Malcolm Cowley writes eulogy in *Saturday Review.*

CHAPTER 1

Life and Letters

I The Early Life

HAMILTON Basso was born in New Orleans on September 5, 1904.[1] His family background and early development mirrored the Southern, yet cosmopolitan, character of his home city; his mother, Louise Calamari Basso, and his father, Dominick Basso, were of Italian descent. His grandfather, Joseph Basso, had emigrated from Genoa, Italy, to New England and later to New Orleans, arriving in the 1880s to open a shoe-repair shop which later grew into a small shoe factory.[2] The Basso family lived upstairs over the business, which Dominick Basso inherited, on Decatur Street in the old French Quarter, the Italian district of the city at that time.

Basso describes the delightful local color of the neighborhood in a series of reminiscence pieces published in the *New Yorker* during the 1950s. The house and its walled garden were as colorful as any in the area, and the boy's pets included a three-foot alligator and a parrot who could whistle arias from *Carmen.* Among his childhood friends were the young toughs of the Quarter, a gang called the "Elysian Fields," as well as the stevedores of the working waterfront on the Mississippi, only a few blocks away. His youth seems to have been uneventful for all his boyish adventures around New Orleans; his only sister, Mary, was born in 1911, and the family sold the business and moved beyond Canal Street to the American section in 1914. Basso steadily progressed from Colton Grammar School to Easton High School to Tulane University; at all levels he was a rather indifferent student, as he himself later admitted, except in the study of history and literature. In 1916, at age twelve, the young Basso won a gold medal in a citywide competition sponsored by the Daughters of the Confederacy for a biographical essay on Louisiana's Confederate General Mouton.[3]

Basso's informal education in the streets of New Orleans probably held more importance for his ultimate development as a writer. In the years when Basso grew up there, New Orleans was perhaps the most unique city in America. The Creole heritage still existed in the older quarters, and, along with the influx of Italians, Irish, and Germans, imparted a cosmopolitan flavor to the town. During these same years New Orleans again was becoming the nation's second seaport and one of the important industrial centers in the South; thus the bustling business and shopping areas around Canal Street were progressively American in attitude. Both these traditions were subsumed in New Orleans's Southern identity; the city had developed after Louisiana statehood in 1812 as the chief port of the old South for both raw cotton and human chattels. The Creole sensibility added a romantic aspect to slavery and miscegenation, but the ugly realities behind the wrought-iron grillwork of the quadroon quarter have been unmasked by modern historians and novelists. Early in the Civil War the city was captured by Union forces, suffering a particularly difficult occupation and Reconstruction. Violence and corruption, the legacies of slavery and defeat, formed public life in the city throughout Basso's residence there, culminating in the regime of Huey Long.

II   *The Literary Life*

Fortunately, the developing city had its better side. New Orleans had always been something of a literary and intellectual center from the time of early Creole writers who imitated the romances of Chateaubriand. When Basso entered Tulane University in 1922, the year which marked the maturity of modern literature with the publication of *The Waste Land* and *Ulysses,* the impact of modernism had reached even to New Orleans. Basso, who spent four years at the university as a prelaw student, was soon a budding man of letters. This transformation was wrought not so much under the influence of his English professors as of the group of local and visiting writers centered around the *Double Dealer,* a literary periodical founded in 1921.[4] The most famous of the names, of course, is William Faulkner's, but Sherwood Anderson, Edmund Wilson, and Oliver La Farge were also members for longer and shorter periods of time. The most prominent local members of the *Double Dealer* group were John McClure, Lyle Saxon, and Roark Bradford, all of whom were associated in one capacity or another with the New Orleans newspapers. When Basso wearied of legal studies, and dropped out of Tulane three months before graduation so that he could be sure of never having to practice law, he easily dropped into journalism, which would become a lifelong profession.[5] At different times he worked on all three of the city's important papers; the *Tribune,* the *Item,* and the *Times-Picayune.*

During this period he kept up his creative writing under the stimulation of William Faulkner's company, after the older writer had returned from his first European sojourn. Faulkner particularly liked Basso because together they had flown with a visiting aerobatic circus.[6] After Faulkner's death Basso would recall wild drinkimg parties and late-night games of drunken tag along the roofs of the French Quarter.[7] Basso was also included in Faulkner and Spratling's satirical volume, *Sherwood Anderson and Other Famous Creoles* (1926), where he is pictured as a very sophisticated young man doing the Charleston with the Muse.

Late in 1926 Basso left New Orleans for New York City. He felt almost obliged to make the journey, for he was at the age when the world appears to be the young man's oyster. Later he said, "But the oyster to my hurt astonishment wouldn't open. Before I got a newspaper job, I had worked in a print shop, trucked freight, and been a salesman in a department store—one of the worst experiences I ever had."[8] Somewhat cooled by his rejection, Basso was back in New Orleans during the great Mississippi flood of 1927.

Yet New Orleans and newspaper work, now with neither the existence of the *Double Dealer* or the presence of Anderson and Faulkner, again became confining for the ambitious young man. First he tried his hand at writing advertising, which he hated passionately. On a trip to New York he imparted this information to Faulkner, who was then in the city finishing *The Sound and the Fury.*[9] The example of the hard-drinking but hard-working young Faulkner, with two novels already to his credit, probably influenced the younger Basso to chuck advertising and return to fiction-writing. In 1929 he was earning a living as a reporter for the *Item* and finishing his first novel, *Relics and Angels,* an autobiographical effort about a young man returning home to New Orleans.

III   *Early Works*

The novel was published by the Macauley Company in New York later that year, the same year which saw the publication of Faulkner's *The Sound and the Fury* and Thomas Wolfe's *Look Homeward, Angel*. These novels marked the full maturity of the Southern Renaissance, of which Basso now became a fledgling member. Basso's book received scant notice, though an old friend from *Double Dealer* days, Edmund Wilson, gave him a favorable review in the influential *New Republic*.[10] Evidently, the lack of critical interest was mirrored in the book's sales, but Basso could take consolation in his friend and fellow novelist's immediate unsuccess with one of America's greatest novels, *The Sound and the Fury*.

Basso must have been confident of future successes because the next year, 1930, he married Etolia Moore Simmons, a local girl he had met at Tulane.[11] In spite of the Depression, the young couple enjoyed life among the intellectuals and artists of the French Quarter, where a good dinner or a bottle of wine was still quite inexpensive. Basso was also advancing in the newspaper world; he moved to the *Times-Picayune*, where he became night city editor briefly. His busy life of this period cut into his creative writing, while the critical and financial failure of *Relics and Angels* weakened his desire to write fiction. He didn't publish another book until 1933, and it was nonfiction, a biography of Confederate General P. G. T. Beauregard.

Basso had always been an avid reader of Southern history, and he was naturally drawn to the colorful Creole general. When he discovered that Beauregard shared his own dislike for Jefferson Davis, the Confederate president, Basso looked further into his career. Finding the only book on Beauregard was decidedly "chocolate coated," he began digging into New Orleans archives and talking to Beauregard's descendants.[12] The product of his research was *Beauregard: The Great Creole,* published by Scribners in 1933. The book was very well received critically, but, unfortunately for its sales, it appeared on the day President Roosevelt closed the banks. This coincidence caused Etolia Basso to remark that the life of a writer resembled the Perils of Pauline.[13]

The Bassos then left New Orleans's Bohemian and newspaper

worlds for a sojourn in the mountains of western North Carolina. Settled at Pisgah Forest near Asheville in a cabin rented for $10 a month, Basso had the leisure to write *Cinnamon Seed,* his second novel.[14] It was published in 1934, by Scribners, where Max Perkins was his editor. A much fuller and stronger effort than his first, the book received generally favorable reviews and enjoyed a modest success. Like *Relics and Angels* it concerns an autobiographical protagonist, but like his later novels of the 1930s it also creates a realistic and liberal portrait of the Depression South. In this latter element it is close to his next novel, published a year later, *In Their Own Image* (1935). At that time Basso had gone back to journalism as an associate editor of the liberal *New Republic.* His duties forced him to move to New York, while his assignments carried him around the country to places like Scottsboro, Alabama, for the famous trial of the Scottsboro boys, and Gastonia, North Carolina, scene of a bitter textile strike. A similar strike forms the background for *In Their Own Image,* set in Aiken, South Carolina, where the Bassos had lived during the winters in a friend's guest house when their mountain cabin got too cold for creativity.[15] The new novel is interesting as the only Basso work without the now-recognizable "Basso protagonist." Social issues, such as the strike, were evidently foremost in the mind of the thirty-one-year-old novelist.

Yet Basso never subscribed to the literary leftism then so strong in American letters. His *New Republic* articles and his novels criticized the failures of the American system, but they as vigorously attacked the false prophets of the far left and the far right. In 1937 he argued with his friend and former editor Malcolm Cowley about literary Marxism: "I can't accept Marx as a Bible, as infallible, when I know goddamn well he *is* fallible."[16] In 1939 Basso summed up what the Depression Decade had taught him about politics.

I am, I suppose, a free-thinking liberal opposed to any kind of dictatorship whether it be of the right or of the left. I believe that America has something that no other country can match—a promise, a hope, call it a dream—and that its potentialities have never been realized. My political opinions, however, are my own, and I don't want to preach them or try to cram them down anybody's throat.[17]

IV *First Success*

While he was producing analyses of public personalities as
diverse as Huey Long and Thomas Wolfe for the *New Republic*,
Basso returned to his autobiographical protagonist in his third
novel in three years, *Courthouse Square*, published by Scribners
in 1936. Basso as novelist came of age with this book, his first
completely successful effort. The Southerner who returns home
in this novel is a sensitive young writer who rails against the
injustice of Southern society and matures as he recognizes his
complicity in it. This time his reviewers were quite positive, and
Basso enjoyed a modest fame as a young Southern writer.

Basso then left the *New Republic*, and though he continued to
freelance his output of articles fell off considerably. He returned
to the North Carolina mountains during this time, buying a house
at Pisgah Forest and renewing his friendship with Thomas
Wolfe.[18] The writers shared many a conversation and bottle, and
it can be speculated that Basso, now moderately comfortable
financially, was taking some time to read and study in order to
renew his intellectual energies. Certainly, his next two novels,
Days Before Lent (1939) and *Wine of the Country* (1941), give
this indication. The first is about a young doctor in New Orleans
who specializes in tropical diseases; the second, about a young
anthropologist from South Carolina. Both fields of study are old
interests of Basso's, but they are brought up to date in the novels
as the books present an objective, scientific view of a world
poised on the edge of its most destructive war. Basso had a
firsthand look at Fascism during a trip to Italy in 1938, and his
uneasiness is reflected in *Days Before Lent,* one of his most
successful novels in terms of critical response. The book won the
Southern Authors Award for 1940 over such competition as
Wolfe's posthumous *The Web and the Rock,* Robert Penn
Warren's first novel, *Nightrider,* and Lillian Hellman's successful
play *The Little Foxes.*[19]

Between the publication of his two intellectual novels, the
Bassos lived for six months in the South of France but returned to
North Carolina for the birth of their only child, Keith, in
Asheville in March of 1940.[20] The following winter was spent in
Charlottesville, Virginia, and Aiken, South Carolina.[21] In 1941
the family moved to South Hadley, Massachusetts, where Basso

finished his novel about an anthropology professor, *Wine of the Country*, which Scribners published in October 1941, directly before Pearl Harbor.

V *The War and After*

Basso tried to enlist, but was excused from military service for family and medical reasons, including poor eyesight.[22] He did weekend work for OSS while serving as a home front journalist for the duration of the war, working first at *Time* magazine (1942-43) and later for the *New Yorker* (1944-61). Some of Basso's best writing was done for the *New Yorker*, including the well-known profiles of Eugene O'Neill and Somerset Maugham, a number of book reviews, and some fine short stories, a form which Basso had virtually neglected until the 1940s. During the war, Basso published one novel, *Sun In Capricorn* (1942), and one nonfiction work, *Mainstream* (1943). The novel, his last with Scribners, is notable for its fictional portrait of Huey Long, which deserves comparison with Warren's *All the King's Men* (1946). *Mainstream* is a series of biographies of representative Americans (including Huey Long) who helped to shape the nation; it is notable for its rather patriotic conclusions.

In 1943 the Bassos moved to Weston, Connecticut, a pleasant town within commuting distance of New York City.[23] After the war the writer continued at the *New Yorker*, and did freelance work, including travel-writing for a number of magazines. In 1948 he provided an introduction for his wife's book, *The World From Jackson Square*, a collection of pieces by various writers about New Orleans. His next novel, *The Greenroom*, did not appear until 1949. It was done by Doubleday, who also published all the rest of his books except his last. Although seen through the perspective of the typical Basso protagonist, the novel is his first to depict really complex feminine personalities. Set in the south of France, it centers on Mrs. Porter, an expatriated American novelist probably modeled after Edith Wharton. Indeed, the novel itself is reminiscent of Wharton's work, or of her master, Henry James. Altogether it is perhaps the most literarily successful of Basso's works; though very well reviewed, it was only a very modest popular success.

VI   *The Pompey's Head Novels*

Basso's next novel, *The View From Pompey's Head* (1954), was his first best-seller. The novel was conceived as part of a Southern trilogy on a visit Basso paid to Savannah, Georgia, in 1951.[24] Basso, perhaps under the influence of the map of Yoknapatawpha County in *The Portable Faulkner*, first made a map of a fictional Pompey's Head and then evolved a history and a personality for the place. Carefully writing over the next several years, Basso polished his favorite situation of the expatriated Southerner returning home into a commercial property, perhaps under the example of John Marquand.[25] Not that the novel is less honest than his other works; it simply extends to an extreme Basso's predilection for popular plotting. The novel, a Literary Guild selection, was well promoted by Doubleday and sold 75,000 copies in hardback; it was printed as a condensed book by *Woman's Home Companion* and *Reader's Digest;* and it went to the movies for a large sum.[26]

The novel's success guaranteed good sales for the second volume of the trilogy, *The Light Infantry Ball*, which appeared in 1959. This novel views Pompey's Head during the Civil War, and it benefits from Basso's thorough knowledge of Southern history. Although dismissed by some critics as an old-fashioned costume romance, the book is actually a realistic historical novel, and one of Basso's better efforts.

These years were the Bassos' happiest, living comfortably in Connecticut, traveling extensively, and watching their son grow up. Keith attended Harvard University, where he majored in anthropology and graduated with honors; later he was to receive his Ph.D. at Stanford, and today is Professor of Anthropology at the University of Arizona.[27] Basso's literary friends in Connecticut included Malcolm Cowley, Van Wyck Brooks, Matthew Josephson, John Hersey, and Peter DeVries, and he also saw old friends like Faulkner as he traveled.[28] Basso had been elected to the National Institute of Arts and Letters, and was a vice president of that organization when Faulkner presented its annual award to John Dos Passos in 1957.[29] When the old friends met they were both well known and well regarded. Faulkner had passed the height of his career, but Basso was still to complete *The Light Infantry Ball.*

VII   *Final Years*

He was fifty-five when this work appeared in 1959. Undoubtedly, he would have had many productive years ahead of him if
he had not been afflicted with serious illness. The author worked
for some time on an unfinished novel set in Tahiti, but he could
never bring it to the right level of polish.[30] During the last five
years of his life Basso published only two more books, *A Quota of
Seaweed* in 1960 and *A Touch of the Dragon* in 1964. The first is
a collection of travel sketches, most of which had appeared
earlier in magazines; the second is one of his less-successful
novels. Undoubtedly it was weakened by his declining powers, as
he took it up after the failure with the Tahiti novel.

Hamilton Basso died on May 13, 1964, at the age of fifty-nine.
His funeral was attended by many literary friends, and Malcolm
Cowley wrote a touching memorial in the *Saturday Review*
which recalled Basso's reminiscence of Faulkner written two
years earlier after his old friend's death.[31]

VIII   *A Southern Writer*

Basso's biography places him, first and foremost, as a Southern
writer, though he lived in the New York area through much of
his career. His personal background and development were
Southern (New Orleans), and most of his novels either are set in
the South (Louisiana and South Carolina), or concern Southerners sojourning in the North. His important literary friendships
were formed in the South, and his most important literary
connections are with William Faulkner (from the days of the
Double Dealer in New Orleans) and later Thomas Wolfe (in
North Carolina) and the exiled Southerners (in Connecticut).
Like Faulkner, Basso created his own fictional world in Pompey's
Head, South Carolina; like Wolfe, he wrote of the exiled
Southerner living in New York and unsuccessfully attempting to
go home again; like Warren, he centered a novel around the
figure of Huey Long. Even more importantly Basso demonstrates
the particular patterns of image and idea which make Southern
literature different from that created in other sections of the
country.

Southern literature is different because the South essentially differs from the other sections of the United States, no matter how much the propaganda of Southern Chambers of Commerce insists on its homogeneity. The country itself is different, contrasting in topography, climate, and cultivation; the semi-tropical weather and the rich, alluvial soil led to the inevitable development of an agricultural economy and an agrarian culture. The patterns of society stayed close to the rhythms of nature, while the absence of cities, machines, and factories allowed the South to remain an area of closed communities where social relationships are codified and ritualized.

Historically considered, these differences alone would be enough to separate the South from the industrialized Northeast and the expanding, dynamic West, but the peculiar development of Southern agriculture in the plantation organization and the slave economy created far deeper differences. C. Vann Woodward's famous essay "The Burden of Southern History" enumerates these deviations: only the South knew the full, sinful sense of human exploitation in slavery; only the South compulsively defended itself from its own guilt feelings through an almost suicidal armed revolt; only the South suffered the ignominy of defeat and tasted the despair of ravagement and military occupation. Thus the history of the South produced an area different from the rest of America in its bondage to history.[32]

In his effort not to despise his own past, the Southerner produced a Myth of Southern history which excused him from the burden of his defeat and his guilt.[33] The popular Southern romance, such as *Gone With the Wind*, is energized by this myth, as are many Southern political, social, and cultural institutions. Critics of the Southern Myth, such as Wilbur J. Cash in his influential study *The Mind of the South*, quickly demonstrate both the shallow view of history evident in the Myth and its paradoxical tenacity in the Southern mind.[34] The Myth fills an emotional, not an intellectual, need, and therefore it is as important to the Southerner as the reality of his history.

Man's ambiguous relation to nature, the claustrophobic isolation of the closed society, the alienation of the black and poor white classes in a stratified economy are the subjects of the Southern fictionist. History, the past, and time itself are often the Southern fictionist's themes. The critics of Southern writing show how man emerges as a fallen, limited creature locked in a prison of loneliness. This literature is a drama of dark complexity marked by a conservative, fiercely moral (almost Calvinistic), and tragic vision of the human, the American, and the Southern conditions. It is especially complex and ambiguous in the fiction of the Southern Renaissance.

These images, themes, and meanings appear and reappear throughout most of the eleven novels which Hamilton Basso produced between 1929 and 1964. First of all, he insists on the separateness, the difference, and the alienation of the South from the rest of the country. He carefully pictures the countryside, the towns, and the cities of the South in relation to natural and human history. He realistically depicts the tightly codified and structured social systems in Southern society. He considers the tragic results of Southern preoccupation with a tragic past, particularly in the Southern attempt to justify the "Myth" historically.

In an important article, "Letters in the South," which appeared in the *New Republic* in 1935, Basso divided the Southern Renaissance into rival camps separated by their attitudes toward the Myth of Southern history.[35] On the one hand were the group he called Southern Realists, the party to which he allied himself; it contained Faulkner, Caldwell, Wolfe, T. S. Stribling, and Grace Lumpkin. In the opposing group were Tate, Ransom, Davidson, Lytle, Warren, Stark Young, Dubose Hayward, Caroline Gordon, and Roark Bradford. The lists are interesting in an historical perspective, and the general differentiation of the two groups as "realists" and "traditionalists" is clear enough. Yet by 1962, when he wrote his eulogy for Faulkner, Basso recognized that his friend was not a realist.

Those who read him as a "realistic" novelist might just as well read Dante as a [Baedeker] to the nether regions, and Milton as a Michelin going in the opposite direction.[36]

Contemporary criticism would also question Wolfe's place in that camp. Rather, Faulkner and Wolfe, along with most of the other important fictionists of the Southern Renaissance, are literary modernists, with more ties to the romance tradition than to the traditional realistic novel. These writers more often employed the gothic and the grotesque in their vision of the Southern wasteland, rather than the realists' objective and scientific view.

IX   A Southern Realist

The realistic vision in modern Southern literature has been less important than the other traditions, but it is still a vital force which is receiving greater recognition today. Starting before the Renaissance in the work of George Washington Cable and Ellen Glasgow, the tradition of Southern Realism was well established during the first decade of the Renaissance by writers such as Elizabeth Maddox Roberts, T. S. Stribling, and Berry Fleming. The Depression Decade of the 1930s, with its resulting social and economic analysis, strengthened this movement in the work of Grace Lumpkin, Olive Dargan, and Hamilton Basso. Later writers such as Burke Davis, Madison Jones, and William Bradford Huie have continued the tradition down to the present day.[37]

Literary modes are difficult to define with precision, but some sense of the nature of Realism is necessary for a full appreciation of Basso's fiction. The critics who have attempted generalizations about American Realism have most often divided their discussion into the three categories: realistic matter, method, and philosophy. George Becker, in his well-known essay on Realism, presents the acceptable idea that the subject matter of realistic fiction emphasizes the commonplace, the regional, and the lower reaches of society.[38] He characterizes realistic method by unusual stress on observation, documentation, and objectivity. Finally, he identifies the philosophy of Realism with common sense, pragmatism, and incipient naturalism. Professor Becker summarizes by presenting Realism as "the truthful representation of observable fact with emphasis on the norm of experience." Until quite recently most discussion of American Realism and the realistic mode in American literature has proceeded from these or similar definitions.

Recent work on Realism has shifted many of these emphases. Donald Pizer's provocative work *Realism and Naturalism in Nineteenth Century American Literature* questions the assumption of commonality in subject matter; after all, the greatest American novelist of the realistic period, Henry James, wrote of a society insulated from ordinary economic reality.[39] Pizer also points out that Twain and Howells presented moral systems which were highly idealistic (in James's case almost ethereal). Harold Kolb is even more iconoclastic in his recent book, *The*

Illusion of Life.[40] In Kolb's view almost all earlier generalizations about Realism are suspect as untested clichés. He proceeds to define the mode by topical, but not necessarily "ordinary," matter, by a liberal and ethical, though unidealized, philosophical overview, and by a characteristic style. This realistic style is marked by antiomniscience, by complexity and ambiguity, by imagery rather than symbolism, and by concern for character rather than action. Professor Kolb tests his theories by connecting them to many disparate works of American Realism and in the process writing excellent criticism of realistic novels.

Basso's fiction certainly seems to fit all these definitions of Realism. It stresses a regional analysis, as his biography indicates; moreover he deals with middle-class society in the South, rather than the extremes of the degenerate aristocracy or the grotesque poor whites and blacks featured in so many modern Southern novels. Quite often Basso considers topical subject matter in his treatment of subjects such as textile strikes or populist demagogues. His philosophical overview is characterized by a common-sense approach to ethical problems and a liberal attitude toward social problems. Basso's newspaper background seems obvious in his objective, reportorial style. The writer made few remarks about his methodology, but one defines a realist's perspective. "Mr. Basso's only theory of fiction, he insists, is to try to say what he means, and to mean what he says."[41] Although most often working in third person, he limits his viewpoint to his central character (almost always the autobiographical "Basso" protagonist), thereby precluding any sense of omniscience on the part of the author. In turn, as omniscience decreases, the levels of ambiguity and complexity increase. His complexity is not that of Faulkner's tortured syntax or ambiguous symbols, but rather that of difficult choices within the areas of personal and social morality. Like most important realistic fiction, Basso's work probes the difficult balance which must be struck between individual and society. Finally, Basso's fiction is much stronger in the presentation of character, especially the autobiographical protagonist, than in organic plotting. In fact, problems of plotting constitute the major difficulty in Basso's fiction, as the analysis of the novels will demonstrate.

In summary, Basso is a novelist of the Southern Renaissance. His novels develop out of his own experience of a defeated, impoverished, and guilt-ridden South, yet his method, unlike that of most Southern novelists, is essentially realistic. He eschews sensationalism, sentimentalism, and gothicism in his presentation of topical problems from a realistic, ethical, and liberal perspective. Although his vision sometimes falters, he is essentially successful in his portrayal of modern Southern life. Thus his work proves both instructive and valuable to the student of both Southern and American letters and life.

CHAPTER 2

The First Novel

"THIS volume is intended as an introduction to certain characters with whom the author intends to concern himself in the future." Thus Hamilton Basso prefaced *Relics and Angels*, his first novel. In all probability the author intended to continue the development of Tony Clezac beyond the ambiguous epiphany at the tent revival which concludes the book. Although Basso never did return to this story, his remark still had more significance than he could have foreseen; in a larger sense Basso returned again and again to Tony Clezac, the prototype of the "Basso protagonist."

It is interesting from both biographical and critical perspectives that Basso was later to reject the firstborn of his literary progeny. Even in the original biographical sketch he submitted for the reference work *Twentieth Century American Authors*, Basso referred to *Relics and Angels* as "a very, very bad first novel."[1] Why he reacted so negatively to the book is difficult to understand. Certainly it is not a very good novel, but it is far from being "very, very bad." In many ways, it is one of his most interesting books, and certainly it contains in embryonic form the characters, plots, settings, and symbols of his later works. Basso's reasons for his rejection were undoubtedly personal and complex, but they would seem to center on the novel's romantic themes and its structural difficulties.

Tony Clezac became a problematical character for Hamilton Basso because he was obviously autobiographical and just as obviously romantic. Like all Basso protagonists, Clezac is intelligent, idealistic, and sensitive; unlike the later variations he is also impressionable, quixotic, and sentimental. To a great extent these differences are simply questions of maturity, both of the character and his creator. Clezac is a twenty-five-year-old version of a character who is most often between thirty and forty

27

in Basso's later books. Here the character suffers all the pangs of unrequited love and unfulfilled ambition. Undoubtedly the author intended much of this fatuousness on the part of his character, but in later years Basso probably detected much that he had not intended. The rejection of the novel was the act of an older writer who had been tempered by the Depression and World War II, by fatherhood and financial problems, to a realistic toughness. Thus Basso was cutting off an element of his writing personality he felt he had outgrown, much as Hemingway and Faulkner rejected their early poetry.

Clezac resembles the younger protagonists already created by Hemingway and Faulkner—Nick Adams and Bayard Sartoris—as well as earlier portraits of incipient artists—Joyce's Stephen Dedalus and Lawrence's Paul Morel. The same year which saw the publication of *Relics and Angels*, 1929, also saw two other sensitive young men appear in American fiction: Quentin Compson in Faulkner's *The Sound and the Fury*, and Eugene Gant in Thomas Wolfe's *Look Homeward, Angel.* Tony Clezac is not a great characterization like these more famous youths, but he is very definitely their spiritual kin. He is a Southerner, though an urban and urbane example; he is from an old and disintegrating family; he is well educated and sensitive to the problems of living in the modern world. All of these characters are faced with the difficulty of finding an order in an orderless world, a place where they can function as creative people. All the Southerners, like Joyce's Stephen and Lawrence's Paul, are alienated from their families and backgrounds by the suffocating constrictions of middle-class life. Of course, Quentin is the greatest failure, committing suicide in his frustration; Eugene is the most successful, for the final chapter of *Look Homeward, Angel* is a vision of artistic success symbolized by the dreamlike movement of the stone angels. Tony is somewhere between these extremes; he is not destroyed by his world, but his dream vision in the final chapter of *Relics and Angels* does not confirm the direction or success of his vocation.

Clezac also stands between young Compson and young Gant in his autobiographical relationship to his creator; Tony is not as close to Basso as Eugene is to Wolfe, though he is probably closer to the twenty-five-year-old Basso, still struggling to find a career, than was the suicidal Quentin to the thirty-year-old Faulkner who created him. Tony Clezac, like Hamilton Basso, was born in New Orleans, the scion of an established family which made its money in shoe manufacturing. The Clezacs' townhouse and its gardens, complete with ruined fountain, are as symbolic as the Sutpen Hundred. Again like Basso, Clezac was educated in public schools and the local university before leaving for travel to New York and Europe. His trip to Rome matured him, for, as in the works of Hawthorne or Henry James, the Eternal City represents the eternal knowledge of human limitations. Tony's mother and father both died when he was quite young; he and his sister, Laurine, were raised by their paternal grandparents. Eventually the grandfather, the founder of the shoe business, left the grandmother for his mistress, and they settled in Rome. Tony left New Orleans to join them and to do further study of bacteriology, his specialty, in the malaria laboratories of Italy. After the grandfather dies suddenly, Tony has returned to New Orleans in order to take care of the rest of the family—his grandmother, his unmarried sister, and his maiden great aunt, Hermine.

The setting of New Orleans is very effectively used for both realistic and symbolic purposes. The careful description of a city known to every tourist undoubtedly adds to the reader's interest, as in Basso's later novel, *Days Before Lent*. However, the city also functions much as Dublin does in Joyce's *Portrait*, as a symbolic equivalent to the central character's states of mind. After arriving home and rediscovering his family's heritage he wanders the streets of the *Vieux Carre*, where the lamps ". . . shed a powdery blue light that transformed the narrow streets and balconied houses into sets for some very sentimental and romantic play" (36). He is taken by more serious thoughts near Jackson Square when he looks on the cathedral. "He began to walk away, thinking, as echoes slipped along mouldering walls, of something that had happened . . . something he had almost forgotten" (37). This passage leads into a long reminiscence of his boyhood religious feelings, especially at Mass, and the whole scene is an important prefigurement of the novel's conclusion. His home, the cathedral, the hospital, the country club, and the factory are all well rendered, and all ultimately evolve into symbols of various human conditions.

Basso opens the novel in the waiting room of the Catholic hospital where his grandmother is now a nurse. This setting is symbolically appropriate because Tony, undergoing a spiritual rebirth, first visits the hospital where he was born a quarter of a century earlier. The first person he meets is the old woman who has been his surrogate mother. Significantly, her religious name is now Mother Annette, as she is now mother superior of the nuns; thus she represents a spiritual guide for the young man.

As Tony waits in the hospital office he sinks back into his memories, finally immersing himself in his deepest sense of selfhood.

Looking into himself, Tony could always remember back of given times. He could remember back of the time when father died, when as a child he sat in the garden, listening to the empty sound of the wind. He could remember back of the time when first he clung to grandfather's thumb, standing on the edge of wharves, spelling out the names of ships.

But never could he remember back of the time when he was not aware of the other, the self within himself, anxiously alive, frequently more alive than himself. (9)

Consciousness of this other self flows freely in response to his physical return and to his spiritual pilgrimage. The hospital is an especially appropriate setting, because to this point, Tony's most serious commitment has been to medical research. In one sense he has come home to his spiritual mother in order to find out which is his true self.

The hospital's director, with his "prelate's stomach" (9), is a false priest of medical science because he thinks only of official reports. The nurse, Miss Cartwright, guides him to Mother Superior, but she is no spiritual guide, smelling only of disinfectant. Even the Sister of Charity, Mother Annette, cannot be an infallible guide, for she is torn between feelings of joy on Tony's arrival and feelings of despair over her husband's desertion and death.

More important to Tony are the messages from the other, deeper self which he receives throughout the chapter. Over half the chapter is devoted to reminiscence of events in Tony's past life, ranging from his earliest memories of life with his grandparents to his recent decision to abandon his medical research. Tony remembers a Sunday meal very similar to the Christmas dinner in Joyce's *Portrait,* where his grandfather, an atheist, argues with his grandmother and grandaunt about the existence of God. The argument had been occasioned by the grandmother's insistence that Tony eat his broth; the grandfather is in a sense rejecting the image of his wife as nurse to the children, as well as her attitude toward religion. Tony also remembers the grandfather in the fullness of his relationship with his mistress, who wears a yellow dress full of sunlight. Just as he was when a child, Tony is confused by the chaos of his many loves and desires: grandmother-grandfather, commitment-freedom, tradition-change.

In Chapter Two he walks from the hospital to his home, still reflecting on his past. The house, of course, symbolizes the whole Clezac tradition, the romantic past and the decadent present. "Some of the houses were altered and some had fallen into decay. But he recognized them all and wondered what had happened to the people who had lived in them" (29). Inside wait Aunt Hermine, old and dying, and his sister, Laurine, young and vibrant; they represent the death of the past and the life of the future. Tony, in the present, is inspired by this reversal of his despondent mood, and, buoyed by his sister's enthusiasm, he thinks again of continuing his medical research.

In Chapter Three the St. Louis Cathedral is used to represent his sense of spiritual vacation. The cathedral's spire in the moonlight leads him to remember youthful experiences as an altar boy and the religious instructions of Father Van Eyck. These experiences are again reminiscent of Stephen Dedalus at Clongowes College, and the priest is as much a surrogate father to Tony as the Jesuits are to Stephen. Tony's train of association connects Father Van Eyck with Professor Hugo Mullendorf, his mentor in the yellow-fever research in Italy. The professor, who was a great friend of Tony's grandfather, has evidently shaped the young man's intellectual position more than any other person. At this point, Tony recalls Hugo's pronouncements on the chain of being and the intertwining of individual destinies. Quite obviously, Tony desperately wants to sort out his personal responsibilities and desires.

In the next chapter, Tony symbolically assumes the family's tradition by arriving for work at the factory. His grandfather had founded the factory almost a half-century earlier, and it had flourished under his guidance to become the largest shoe manufactory in the South. In those years the factory had been a place of craftsmanship; now it has become a place of mass production under the new manager, Mr. Epstein. Even the name is changed from Clezac's to Forward Shoes. Yet Tony's name is being gilt-lettered on an office door, and a portrait of the grandfather is hung in the manager's office. Tony tries hard to fit into Epstein's forward-looking boosterism, finally failing much as Quentin Compson fails at Harvard or Eugene Gant fails at magazine sales.

The country club becomes the symbolic setting of Tony's social failure in Chapter Five. His sister takes him to the Sunday-afternoon gathering of the "fast" set around the club's elegant pool. Although the assembled company accepts him for his sister and his position, Tony finds it impossible to communicate with them. They tell pointless "in" jokes and employ "jive" slang which he simply doesn't understand. Soon their conversation degenerates into drunken inanity; as at some party in Fitzgerald's fiction, everyone talks but no one listens. Tony isn't turned on even by the attentions of the attractive young girls present, and he decides to lose himself in the pool.

His plunge takes him from the "wasteland" world of the young crowd deep into another symbolic world, one reminiscent of T. S. Eliot's pervasively influential poem published in 1922. As Tony swims the bottom of the pool he repeats "Full Fathom Five." Earlier Tony remembers the lines of Ariel's song from *The Tempest* when holding a seashell, a relic of his boyhood visits to the beach.

> Full fathom five thy father lies;
> Of his bones are coral made;
> Those are pearls that were his eyes. . . .

The "Death By Water" section of Eliot's poem repeats the final line, and hints at salvation through sea change. The novel's use of the image becomes very complex because Tony's father had drowned, perhaps a suicide, a year after his wife's death. Furthermore, Tony best remembers Ariel's song on the lips of the "Madame," the grandfather's mistress. Death and sexual love are inextricably and ambiguously intertwined in Tony's deepest consciousness, and like Faulkner's adolescent Quentin he longs for easeful death by water.

In a metaphorical sense he dives deep into his own sub-conscious, by running away from the city to the Gulf Coast beaches of his youth. Here the scenery is manipulated sym-bolically much in the manner of Hemingway, particularly in the stories of *In Our Time* (1924). Tony visits a coastal island, a sandbank balanced between cypress swamp and saltwater of the gulf. In antebellum days this nearly-empty spit had been the most popular resort on the coast, but during the height of the season a hurricane had swept over the island in destructive fury, drowning the vacationers by the score. Tony reacts to this scene of death by dreaming of the swamp—dark and impassable. In it he discovers the image of a malformed bear.

> Tony's feet sink in the mud. Cypress fingers would have his eyes. The dart of a moccasin is close to his feet. Fires spring up and wrap dark bracelets about the trees.
> He comes across a malformed bear. It sits on its haunches. Its tongue hangs out. It licks itself. The bear is a cub unto itself.
> Millions of years will pass. Winds will cease and suns grow cold. Stars will fall and mountains collapse. But the bear will not take shape.
> A branch snaps beneath his feet. Its ends are bubbles in the mire. Slowly the bear turns. Slowly it looks at him. Slowly fury stains its eyes. Slowly it comes toward him. (74)

The bear seems analogous to Tony himself, half-formed. In the swamp it will never be fully formed, but in the sunlit ocean, Tony feels fully alive, "surrendering his body to the willing embrace of the sea" (81). In the midst of this renewing immersion of the sea, Tony meets the island's other visitor, an attractive young woman named Helen Montross.

As soon as Basso introduces the significantly named Helen, his characterization, plotting, and symbolism begin to get away from him. Part One of the novel, the return to New Orleans and to Tony's personal past, is very nicely handled; Part Two, the return to the seacoast, is nicely conceived but poorly handled. First there is too much coincidence and too little motivation. Helen is the wife of a childhood enemy of Tony's, Bill Montross. In an awkward flashback chapter, Basso has Helen reminisce about her seduction of the well-to-do Bill. Not only does this chapter fail to advance the plot; it demonstrates an extremely shallow portrait of feminine psychology.

Basso would always have difficulty with his feminine characters, particularly his younger women, but Helen Montross is a completely implausible characterization. On the one hand the reader is asked to believe that she callously marries Montross for his money, and then sensitively retreats to the deserted island to contemplate her action. There she allows Tony to make love to her, though later she repents and returns to Bill, and all with no motivation; she has nothing in common with Tony, less even than she does with Montross, and even less is there any reason for Tony to fall romantically in love with her, except that he is lonely and needs a woman. Basso symbolically suggests his biological urges by having him help in the birth of a baby to one of the island's Cajun women, but the Tony of this affair is more silly than sensitive, more quixotic than idealistic.

In Part Three he receives his comeuppance. Back in the city Helen quickly adjusts to reality and sees that from this perspective her affair with Tony is more frightening than exciting. Everything about Tony, from his driving to his demeanor, scares her away from him. On a later excursion, out into the cane country, she again yields to his importuning; yet again returned to town she resolves to break with him. Tony all this time refuses to recognize the signals which even the dullest of readers could not look past. She rejects motherhood; she fawns on society; she hates blacks. Yet Tony sees nothing, and Basso's prose turns as flat as this failure in characterization. "The idea that Helen had married Montross for tawdry purposes of her own, never came to him. If it had, he would have dismissed it immediately" (93).

Many of the subsidiary characterizations and subplots in this section of the novel are handled with considerable skill. On the trip to the country, the lovers encounter an old black woman who is as wise as Faulkner's Dilsey, and Basso contrasts the simple but faithful love of the woman for her husband and son with Helen's faithlessness to both Bill and Tony. When Helen finally reveals herself—significantly, at a country-club dance—by refusing to run off after the example of his grandfather and his mistress, Tony recoils with hurt and shock.

In Part Four he receives another shock; he loses his job at the factory. Earlier, Mr. Epstein had asked Tony to make a speech at the factory workers' monthly meeting, and Tony readily agreed because he wanted to reach the men. His speech, a sort of sentimentalized version of Henry Adams's "The Dynamo and the Virgin," leaves the men more puzzled than moved. One union organizer mistakes the sentiment involved and attempts a wildcat strike in light of the imagined management support. The strike falls apart immediately, but the board of directors suspects

Tony of leftist leanings and subsequently demands his resignation. Tony happily complies because, as the speech indicates, he really understands nothing of American industry.

This whole subplot, aside from the speech itself, which shows Tony's attempt to spiritualize the mechanical world, is rather poorly done. As with Tony's love relationship, it is very difficult for the reader to accept this degree of naiveté in the character. The whole sequence of the strike and the board's reaction seems contrived to get Tony out of the factory rather than to comment on his ideas or on modern industrial society. Basso will make a real advance in social comment in his next three novels, which were tempered by the economic strife of the 1930s.

In Part Four Tony drifts aimlessly about the city, trying to evolve some plan of action. His wanderings again take him past the cathedral, where he stops and meditates about his future possibilities. Now, in the middle of January, Tony weathers the winter of his discontent.

> It was not to be supposed, as he sometimes told himself, that he would be able to return to that peculiar identity which he possessed upon returning to his own country. Many months had passed, there had been adventures and encounters, some discordant, some pleasant, and he had been changed.
>
> There had come, for one thing, the beginning of personal distrust. The blind faith in the eventual outcome of his own destiny was no longer there. Where there had been only roots of certainty there now sprang seedlings of doubt. (180)

Tony is truly discovering the lesson learned by Thomas Wolfe, that one can't go home again. Yet a reverie connects his future with his immediate and distant pasts. He daydreams of himself as a priest in black vestments preaching an incoherent sermon about Judas to an uncomprehending multitude. The black vestments prove appropriate, for the next morning Aunt Hermine is very ill, and within a few days she is close to death. Mother Annette moves back to the Clezac home to nurse her; at first her care seems to revive the old lady, and everyone is relieved.

Tony goes out for a change of scenery and runs into Peter Slade, one of the workmen from the factory, and another childhood friend, in a working-class tavern where he stops for a sandwich. The chance meeting with Slade initiates the major development of Part Four, an affair with the young man's sister, Marianne Slade. As with the Helen Montross episode, motivation is a major difficulty here. Although it is easy to suppose that Marianne would be attracted to the "classy" young Clezac, why he responds to her, even granted his lonely state, seems problematic. And, once again, the picture of the woman is more caricature than characterization, even down to the dialect spellings used in Marianne's dialogue.

Tony's friendship with the Slades does allow Basso to develop several new and interesting parts of the city, which he slowly evolves toward symbolic importance in Part Five. The Slade family's flat is contrasted to the Clezac home, and the taverns and dancehalls which they frequent are the working-class analogues of the country club. In these careful parallelings Basso's methodology is again reminiscent of Eliot's *The Waste Land*, where the poet contrasts the neurotic rich woman with the harridan in the pub. Certain parts of these scenes are also quite close to William Faulkner's picture of New Orleans as wasteland in his second novel, *Mosquitoes.* In particular, Basso's description of the dance on the excursion ship *Reverie* (i.e., the dream) seems indebted to his friend's earlier work. This scene and the midnight supper of soft-shell crabs in the Slades' flat are really very well realized.

Tony is wrenched back to reality by Aunt Hermine's sudden death, and, of course, he bitterly regrets the affair with Marianne. In Part Five, a month after his aunt's funeral, Tony finally starts to pull himself together. He writes to Professor Mullendorf, requesting a position in his laboratory; he soon receives an affirmative reply, though he must postpone the trip back to Italy for his sister's wedding. With Laurine married to another sensitive young man, Ian, and his grandmother back in the hospital's convent, Tony feels he will at last be able to seek his mature responsibility. He also draws closer to a mature sexual relationship in his developing feeling for Camilla Thorne, Laurine's bridesmaid. Camilla, like Laurine, remains an insubstantial figure, the sort of "nice" girl who appears at the right time in several Basso novels, so that her development does little to offset the awkward portraits of Helen Montross and Marianne Slade. In any case, Tony forgets Camilla in the turmoil which ensues when Marianne Slade tells him she is pregnant.

Basso carefully demonstrates that Tony cannot be the baby's

real father, but, again romantically, Tony immediately assumes that he must be. Gallantly he offers to marry her or at least support the child; all Marianne wants is fifty dollars for an abortion. Tony talks her out of it momentarily, but she later goes through with the plan on her own, crushing Tony as if he were the tiny fetus. He had hoped this new life would balance Aunt Hermine's death, and thus he feels completely without hope or life.

He reacts to Marianne's news by getting absolutely drunk and wandering the city once again. In the novel's last chapter he happens into a black revival service and listens to the preacher's message. This conclusion, which is reminiscent of Faulkner's first novel, *Soldiers' Pay* (1926), allows Basso to dramatically sum up his character's confusions. Then he falls into a drunken sleep which is fraught with surrealistic dreams. Finally, he recognizes the vault of the cathedral; an altar boy rings the bells of the consecration and the young priest turns around to bless the multitude. The novel ends with the sentence, "He recognized, in the shadowy figure of the priest, a later portrait of himself" (286).

At least one critic sees this image as indicative of Tony's return to religion as a priest of the Catholic church.[2] Such a reading does not allow enough symbolic play; the reader must remember that the location of this image is in Tony's drunken dream. Therefore it seems more likely that Basso intends the role of the priest as an indication of mature responsibility accepted on Tony's part. Knowing that he cannot return to his childhood past, symbolized by his earlier role as altar boy in the cathedral, Tony must accept the realities of love (Helen, Marianne, Camilla) and death (Grandfather Clezac, Aunt Hermine, Marianne's baby), and ultimately return to his real spiritual father, Dr. Mullendorf, and to his research.

The dream's confirmation of his direction, as well as the title's imagery of angels, connects the book with Wolfe's novel of the same year, *Look Homeward, Angel*. These connections are probably fortuitous; more influential on the novel are Joyce's *Portrait* and Faulkner's early novels *Mosquitoes* and *Soldiers' Pay*. Yet the book is more than a pastiche of current ideas and images. It presents a well-realized autobiographical protagonist, a well-handled setting, and many well-developed image patterns.

In all these areas of success, the book leans toward Basso's basic realism, but it falters in other areas which Basso will strengthen in later novels. Under the influence of Joyce and Faulkner, *Relics and Angels* is Basso's most obvious attempt at literary Modernism. One reviewer complained that the book attempted too much stream of consciousness, for example.[3] The topical material of the labor problems are also handled in the modernist manner, through a long intellectual analysis rather than realistic description. More problematically, several characters intended to be realistic are more symbolic in the final analysis. Basso had not yet fully discovered his realistic material and mode.

For a first novel by a twenty-five-year-old author, *Relics and Angels* is an estimable work, and it was hailed as such by Edmund Wilson in his *New Republic* review. Wilson gives a good summation of the novel's weaknesses and strengths:

. . . rather immaturely conceived and rather vaguely constructed, it still has a grace, a charm, and a distinction which seem to mark the author as an artist, rather than just another young man who has written a novel.[4]

Other, more specific criticism could be added. Some of the subsidiary characters, especially the women, are poorly realized; plotting is mechanically handled; style occasionally becomes turgid. The sensitive reader comes away with a sense of incoherence and of underwriting. *Relics and Angels* is not the "very, very bad first novel" Basso later called it, but it is still obviously a first novel. The writer did not return to the novel form for almost five years, when he had matured sufficiently to create a much better novel, *Cinnamon Seed* (1934).

CHAPTER 3

The Social Novels

I   Cinnamon Seed

*C*INNAMON *Seed* is Basso's first mature work; written in 1933, it appeared in 1934. Five years had passed since *Relics and Angels;* in this time Basso had married, advanced in his journalistic career, and written his successful biography of Beauregard. All of these pursuits had matured him: he understood himself better; he had more material to employ; and he had acquired the habit of careful workmanship. These factors would improve his second novel. Dekker Blackheath is a better rounded and more mature version of the Basso protagonist first recognized in Tony Clezac. The novel narrates a fuller range of the character's experiences, including a great deal of his social observation which can be attributed to Basso's liberal newspaper-writing in the early 1930s. Finally, the novel is much better crafted in terms of plot, structure, and style. In *Cinnamon Seed* Basso fulfilled his realistic bent; the novel concerns topical Southern problems, within a liberal frame of reference, through a complex but careful fictional consideration.

The resemblances to *Relics and Angels,* however, are many and obvious. Dekker Blackheath is at least a literary first cousin to Tony Clezac; like the earlier protagonist he is sensitive, intelligent, and idealistic, but unlike Tony, the adult Dekker is realistic, tough-minded, even cynical. He has seen more of the world, and he is less awed by it. Dekker is more Joyce's Stephen Dedalus of *Ulysses* rather than *Portrait,* more akin to Lawrence's Birkin of *Women in Love* than his Paul Morel of *Sons and Lovers.* The development of the Basso protagonist also parallels the maturing vision contained in the works of William Faulkner and Thomas Wolfe, particularly Faulkner's *Light in August* (1932) and Wolfe's *Of Time and the River* (1936). Again, Basso's book is not as fine as these masterworks of the Southern Renaissance, but, as with the earlier novel, it displays characteristics which make comparison profitable. Like the protagonists created by more famous writers, Dekker Blackheath discovers that no man is an island, that the sensitive young man cannot isolate himself from the demands of the world in adolescent self-pity.

Dekker, like Tony, is a Southern version of this developing character; although born in New Orleans, he grows up on the Blackheath family plantation, Willswood House. Names are important here. Cinnamon seed is a Southern spice, and it is also mentioned in the verses of "Dixie" ("Way down South in the Land of Cotton/Cinnamon Seed and Sandy Bottom"). "Dixie" is reputed by scholars to be Louisiana, land of the "dixs" or ten-dollar bills printed by the Bank of New Orleans. Thus the novel's setting takes on the symbolic sense of the entire South, both geographically and historically, as it does so often in the work of Faulkner and other Southern writers concerned with the movement of Southern history. Like Faulkner's plantations, "Willswood" is an ambiguous piece of property; on the one hand it is beautiful, fecund, rich; on the other it is corrupt, doomed, morally bankrupt. Like Faulkner's Sutpen, the original Blackheath had wrested this garden from the primal woods by his power of will and then willed it to his progeny. But his willfulness in displacing the Indians, enslaving the blacks, and exploiting the poor whites has rendered this inheritance morally suspect.

Dekker Blackheath inherits the name, a typically Southern one which connects the character not just with the rich, alluvial soil of the plantation, but also with the impulsive wildness of primal nature (in particular, Emily Brontë's Heathcliff.) Like many Faulknerian characters, Dekker is the scion of an old, distinguished, and distintegrating Southern family; he is well read and quite sensitive to the world around him, especially to the problem of finding order in a fractioned modern existence.

Like Tony Clezac, Dekker Blackheath was orphaned early, and in his case there is more than just a suspicion of his father's suicide. Kinloch Blackheath put a bullet in his brain in despondency over his wife's death, his subsequent drinking problems, and his failure as a lawyer. The suicide, of course, confirms his failure as a man, a failure with which young Dekker must come to terms. Without a strong role model the young man must struggle to grow into full maturity himself; the novel is basically the story of that struggle.

Unlike Tony Clezac, or other Basso protagonists, Dekker's development is presented on three different chronological levels. In Book One, his father has just committed suicide; Dekker is fourteen years old and entering high school. Book Two begins when he quits college in his senior year, making him about twenty-one. Between Book Two and Book Three Dekker wanders about the South for nearly a decade, and he is about thirty when he returns to Willswood and the novel ends. Basso's narrative strategy makes for some interesting writing; in his other books he often flashes back to his protagonist's youth, but he never treats him as a boy. Over a third of this novel concerns the teenaged Dekker, allowing Basso to use his own New Orleans boyhood to good account. Many of the colorful autobiographical details which Basso recounted later in his reminiscences published by the *New Yorker* appear in the young life of Dekker Blackheath. The Dekker of Book Two corresponds most closely with Tony Clezac from the first novel. In Book Three Dekker achieves the sort of hard-won maturity exhibited by later Basso protagonists, who are all between thirty and forty in these other novels. In the chronological ordering of the central character's life, *Cinnamon Seed* becomes a transition between *Relics and Angels* and his later novels.

This more comprehensive picture of his protagonist also allows its author to extend the complicated relationship of the central character to his family. For example, Dekker's grandfather, Langley Blackheath, is still alive in Book One and his reminiscence allows Basso to portray the family history and the crisis of the Civil War. This background is much more than local color, because the past shapes the present as inexorably as fate. Even the pattern of family relationships is repeated generation after generation. The family fortunes and Willswood plantation were established by Robert Blackheath, Dekker's great-great-grandfather, the first Blackheath, who came from Kentucky for the Battle of New Orleans and stayed as a planter. His son, also Robert, built Willswood House, the prototypical Southern Gothic Mansion in 1850 after he quadrupled his fortune by using guano in the cane fields for the first time. He had two legitimate sons, Edward and Langley, and one illegitimate daughter by his slave mistress, Bella. Edward was his generation's wild, impulsive

Blackheath, riding off to join Bedford Forrest's army at the outset of the War Between the States; he was killed later in a reckless charge at Petersburg. Langley joined later, served less brilliantly, and survived to hold the family together after his father's death in 1865. The relationship of the brothers was repeated in his family; Kinloch, the suicide, recalls Edward; Carter Blackheath became a successful New Orleans lawyer, saving the family as the plantation declined. Langley also has two daughters, Olivia and Ann, who live on in genteel poverty on the plantation, and he provides for the family of his unacknowledged black sister. Dekker continues in the wild tradition of his father, while his cousin John, Carter's son, goes to private schools, Eastern colleges, and, finally, into a successful advertising business in New Orleans, Although the boys do not know it, their black friend, Sam, is actually their cousin.

Thus the relationships of the past shape the relationships of the present. The genealogy is very similar to Faulkner's McCaslin family who appear in the stories of *Go Down, Moses* (1942). The sinful forebear establishes the plantation and the primal curse through exploitation, then the land and the sin are passed down the generations. Edward ran off to embrace death in battle, Kinloch committed suicide, and Dekker must make his adjustment to his family's and his region's past.

The adjustment is more of a struggle as Dekker refuses to accept the two alternatives offered by his family—a genteel accommodation with the past, represented by his Aunt Olivia, or a materialistic accommodation with the present, represented by his Uncle Carter.

In Book One he is essentially in the world of Carter Blackheath, the successful New Orleans attorney, when Carter takes him in, reluctantly, after his father's suicide. The novel opens with Carter's wife, Elizabeth, a sour Northern woman lecturing the young boy on his father's weakness and sinfulness. Later Dekker discusses the conversation with his cousin John while they perform a play Dekker has written, *Lord Byron and the Greeks*, in their puppet theater. Dekker takes the Byronic position, defending his father, suicide, and rebellion while rejecting Aunt Elizabeth, the Bible, and religion. He leaves John and wanders the streets of the French Quarter and the docks along the Mississippi with his street friends, like Pat O'Toole, the son of a policeman, who takes a pragmatic attitude toward death.

The first chapter establishes the direction of Dekker's development throughout the novel; he is always running away from the Blackheaths, trying to find some better wisdom among other people. He runs away from the Carter Blackheaths, in a sense, by asking to spend the summers at Willswood plantation. But even here, he is constantly running off to be with the black and poor-white children who lead more adventurous lives. With his black friend, Lance, he attends a revival meeting, where one woman tears her clothes off in a religious frenzy. Dekker is upset by the sexual suggestions of her act, and by his ambivalent feelings toward the blacks. One of the problems he instinctively senses is his need to understand the relationship of the races. One person he asks is Sam, the family's young retainer, who is actually Robert Blackheath's grandson by Bella, his black mistress. Sam tells him that the blacks are an oppressed people and reveals his plans to go North. Later Dekker and Lance have a vicious fight with the Sturkins, a large family of "white trash" mossgatherers who throw rocks at Lance because he is "a nigger." Dekker can't understand how people can harbor such senseless hate, but it doesn't stop him from having a childish affair with the Sturkins' sluttish sister when the opportunity presents itself. At the end of the summer his grandfather, Langley Blackheath, dies, and his Aunt Ann marries Doctor Tate and moves away to Minneapolis. Dekker matures through his observation of love and death.

The next year Dekker goes to public high school, refusing Carter's offer to send him to a fine military academy with John. Dekker likes the public school better because he can stay with his friends, the Irish and Italian boys of the Quarter. In high school they perform the usual exploits, and Dekker has to talk himself out of several scrapes. It is the same thing in college, again the local institution for Dekker, while John goes off to the Ivy League. Book Two opens when Dekker quits college after a fight with Uncle Carter over his expenses. With nowhere else to go he returns to Willswood to become overseer on the plantation. Here, for several years, he loses himself in the movement of the seasons and the growth of the cane crops.

And there came moments, after hours of heat and sun, when he seemed to move beyond the reach of ordinary human consciousness; when there was nothing but the sun and the motion of the horse

between his thighs and the sweat rolling down his back. All active
consciousness ceased. There were no thoughts, no doubts, no question-
ings. There was no past and no future. There was only the moment,
sharp and dry, and the sweat rolling down and the negroes working in
the cane. In such moments he was content. (174)

He cannot stay content with this essentially mindless life,
however, and the old wildness takes him out to beer joints and
roadhouses. Dekker is almost killed in a drunken auto accident,
and only a few months later he is reinjured in a café brawl. He
then decides that he must live a more orderly life, and again like
Tony Clezac, he tries to order himself in a relationship with a
young woman, in this case Jonquil Keith, a college classmate of
John's fiancée. The girl, called Jonco by her friends, is an
attractive and serious person, rather one-dimensional in the way
of Basso heroines. She is obviously attracted to Dekker, but he is
hesitant in his approach to her. Her family is wealthy, and he has
no real prospects for the future as he doesn't actually own the
plantation. Finally, at a dance honoring John and Constance's
engagement, he has enough of her phony social world, much like
Tony Clezac at the vapid parties in the first novel, and he rejects
her.

In Book Three, Dekker is on the road, tramping the
Depression South and trying to find himself among the ordinary
folks he works with. His jobs include driving a bakery truck,
pulling the green chain in a lumber mill, scrubbing hides in a
tannery, driving a train in a clay mine, and pumping gas at a
roadside garage. None of this satisfies him, either, as he knows
that he is not really part of the working class.

Not in that sense of the word. You don't become a workingman just
by working for a time in a lumber mill or a tannery. These people who
run around trying to identify themselves with the working class,
declaiming that they belong to the proletariat—they always seem a
little futile and cowardly to me. Why are they ashamed by being what
they really are? You can't make yourself a member of the working class
by saying you are any more than you can make yourself a member of
the English aristocracy. I can't kid myself like that. I'm just what I am.
(300–301)

Dekker is still sympathetic with the proleteriat, however, and he
flirts with the Communist party, before deciding, much like

Basso himself, that it is just another orthodoxy, as bad as the ones he is already stuck with. In fact he knows that eventually he must return to Willswood and find his future by confronting his past.

> You told yourself you didn't give a damn about going back, that it all belonged to a part of you that was dead and gone and buried, but that made no difference either. No matter what you said, no matter what you did, sooner or later you went back. You couldn't get out of it. You went back home. (338)

When he does return he faces two immediate crises, both involving his relationships with the plantation's blacks. In the years that Dekker was away Sam has been drawn back to the plantation from New Jersey; like Dekker he knows that he must face up to his fate in the world which has made him what he inevitably is. Unfortunately, the heavy weight of racial hatred pulls him down to ultimate destruction. He has a fight with one of the Sturkin brothers, now a bar owner, and is nearly lynched. Then Dee Dee, his fatherless young cousin, almost causes the death of Elinor, Aunt Ann's daughter who is visiting from Minneapolis; Dee Dee also fears white justice, and in trying to climb into the attic to hide, falls to his death from Willswood's peaked roof. This is too much for Sam, who despairs of personal or racial salvation and hangs himself. Dekker identifies with both characters, Dee Dee because he is a bitter orphan striking out at the world, Sam because he is a mature man trying to live in the nightmare of Southern history. He is crushed when they die, followed soon after by Horace, the family's ancient coachman. Yet the return of spring and the growing cane reassure him that at least life goes on, and he settles again to manage the plantation. In the novel's last chapter he hears that Jonquil Keith is coming for a visit with John and Constance. Basso leaves the impression, much as in the conclusion of *Relics and Angels,* that his character has at least a vision of future maturity.

> Dekker walked toward the fields, his teeth still clenched, something deep and bitter on his face. But suddenly, like a fort of sand built too near the water's edge, all his fury collapsed within him. It left him empty for a moment, filled with a sense of desolation, unconsoled by the clarity of his mind. He was caught, webbed by all the many snares of life, and there was nothing he could do. Behind the house Jeff Davis worked the pump, the handle rattling and the water sloshing into the

pail, and from the cabins the voices of children rose thin and quarrelling on the sunlit air. They shrilled their quarrel out and then there was only the sing-song of the pump and the glittering afternoon drawing subtly to its close. Splashes of sunlight fell upon the house and from the fields there came the scent of growing cane. (378-79)

Dekker Blackheath's story thus proves to be a more mature and complex version of Tony Clezac's, while the several subplots of the novel give *Cinnamon Seed* an even greater scope and complexity. These complementary stories can be divided into three main areas. The historical depiction of the Blackheath family from about 1850 to 1865; the stories of the family's black retainers; and the story of Harry Brand, "The King-Frog of the Pond," a demagogic Louisiana politician. All three stories are integrated at many points with Dekker's story, but they essentially remain materials separate from Dekker's personal development.

The Blackheath genealogy has been sketched above and compared with the complex family histories which Faulkner creates for his troubled characters. However, Langley Blackheath's reminiscences take up about a third of Book One, and constitute an interesting story line in their own right. In one sense, Langley in his development between 1850 and 1865 parallels Dekker between the opening and closing of the whole novel. In 1850, when Langley was just younger than the fourteen-year-old Dekker, his father purchased a beautiful, "high yellow" mistress in New Orleans. A few years later he was present when his mother discovers Robert Blackheath in the cabin with Bella and accuses him of fathering the mulatto child attributed by the plantation folk to Peter Brand, the Northern slave driver. Later both brothers, Edward and Langley, run away to the war, and their adventures are described in considerable detail. Some of this material undoubtedly grew from Basso's research into the Civil War for the Beauregard biography, and it seems somewhat out of place here as it does not directly affect the family history. After Appomattox, Langley returns home to find his father dying, his mother embittered, Peter Brand lording it over the plantation, and Bella living with the Yankee troopers. On the night of Robert Blackheath's death, Bella is cavorting with the soldiers, and in a final rage Mrs. Blackheath shoots her with Langley's cavalry pistol. Langley accepts the blame to shield her, but Peter Brand gives testimony against Mrs. Blackheath, who is convicted, though only fined for her offense. The curse of Cain is on the family, however, and they never recover their former ascendency.

Bella's daughter lives on, and her grandson, Sam, figures prominently in Dekker's story as a slightly older, black surrogate figure for the white protagonist. Several other black characters are developed in the novel, some in the historical sequence, like Jube, the faithful retainer who dies in the field with Edward, and several in the modern history of the family. The most prominent of these are Horace, Jube's son, who is the family's ancient coachman; Emma, Horace's daughter, and the family cook; Lance, Emma's son and Dekker's boyhood friend; and Dee Dee, another son of Emma's, by an unknown father. All of these characters are realistically developed; in fact, several reviewers thought the novel's best feature was its careful and sympathetic handling of black people. Today, Basso's excessive use of dialect seems a little grating, and some of the characters, particularly Horace, verge on stereotyping. The material in Horace's sections consist mainly of his efforts to marry again after his wife's death, and he pays court to a "Madame Queen" type who bilks him out of his savings. Lance, who prefers playing the mouthharp to raking the yard as a boy, grows up to be a bandleader, a development which seems a bit much by contemporary standards. Despite such lapses, Basso's blacks do seem human and real. They do demonstrate the primary Southern problem of racial exploitation, and they do illustrate, particularly in the tragic figures of Sam and Dee Dee, the reality of Southern guilt feelings.

The history of the Brand family shows the result of exploiting the poor whites. Like Faulkner's Snopeses, the Brands (who perhaps carry the brand of Cain as "niggerdrivers") rise to prominence with the failure of the plantation aristocracy, essentially through their ability to function with no guilt feelings at all. Peter Brand got a part of the plantation as a sharecrop farm; his son bought the land; and his grandson, Harry, worked his way off the land through law school, and into a partnership with Carter Blackheath in a powerful New Orleans firm. Using this as a political base he soon is governor and then senator; his career, of course, mirrors the meteoric rise of Huey Long in the real Louisiana politics which Basso covered as a New Orleans reporter. In case we miss the connection, Basso calls his character "Kingfrog" and creates a parallel for every important event in Long's life up to 1934. Although Brand's demagogic career seems the wages of sin for the South, he really fits only peripherally into the Blackheath story, and he may have been intended more to sell the novel than advance its unity. However, he is a well-drawn character, a more temperate version of Long than the evil Gilgo Slade of Basso's later novel *Sun In Capricorn* (1942). The full significance of Long for Basso's fiction will be taken up in connection with the later novel.

James E. Rocks, the most perceptive critic of Basso's work, calls *Cinnamon Seed* the author's most enjoyable and satisfying novel.[1] Certainly it is one of Basso's most interesting and best-written works. The novel presents an appealing figure of the Basso protagonist, who is developed from youth to maturity with more scope and skill than in any of his other personifications. At the same time, the rich profusion of background materials and subsidiary characters creates a true Southern panorama which deserves comparison with the best of Faulkner and Wolfe. It is not suggesting too much to consider the novel's possible influence on Faulkner in the final conception of *Go Down, Moses* (1942); in all probability, Faulkner would have read his friend's first successful novel and would have been impressed by correspondences with his own purposes.

The novel's broad canvas is perhaps its greatest difficulty also. Basso's consistent novelistic problems were proportion and form, and in *Cinnamon Seed* he has too much material to integrate into his central story. In particular, the Civil War materials, Horace's "blackface" antics, and the Harry Brand subplot are hard to justify in terms of the central purpose. The conclusion, with its suggestion of a conventional romantic ending with Dekker and Jonquil living happily ever after on Willswood plantation, also seems forced. Dekker does go through a dark night of the soul after the deaths of Sam and Dee Dee, and the book does suggest that the primary value is to be found in the Southern land itself. All the same, this seems an easy way out of the social questions raised; the poor whites don't own any plantations to return to; the blacks are left still picking cotton or playing the trombone in jazz bands; and the Indians from whom the land was taken are off scratching a subsistence from the scrubby hills of Oklahoma. The reader wants a conclusion with the mature complexity of the

McCaslins' dilemma in *Go Down, Moses.* Yet for all these very real problems, *Cinnamon Seed* is a considerable accomplishment for the second novel of a thirty-year-old novelist, and it points forward to the solid accomplishments of Basso's nine other novels.

II In Their Own Image

In Their Own Image (1935) springs directly from Basso's experiences in the early 1930s as an observer of textile strikes and of the social set in Aiken, S.C. Yet it demonstrates considerably less autobiographical emphasis than his first two novels. This new relationship between the author's life and his fiction accounts for both the strengths and the weaknesses of this third novel. On the one hand the book is more objective, while on the other it is less emotional, intense, and penetrating. *In Their Own Image* proves an interesting book, particularly for the student of Basso's fiction, but it is not one of his more successful novels. It is weakened by too much detachment, too many dull characters, and a perennial Basso difficulty, the forced conclusion of the plot.

The novel's central character is not a "Basso protagonist" but Pierson James, a fifty-nine-year-old advertising executive from New York. His name, perhaps, gives an indication of Basso's intentions in the novel. In spite of the Southern setting, in Aiken, S.C., a wintering place for the "horsey set," and nearby mill towns, *In Their Own Image* is not really a study of the South like *Cinnamon Seed;* rather it advances international themes in its contrasts of American and European characters. In theme, as well as in its ethical stance and Realistic style, the novel recalls the work of America's greatest novelist of manners, Henry James. The novelist of manners essentially attempts to dramatize his world by emphasizing the social relationships of his characters, and this is Basso's purpose in his third novel. His first two books had done some social observation of a similar sort; in particular, the vapid social life at the country club in *Relics and Angels* and at the engagement party in *Cinnamon Seed* prefigure Basso's disgusted and satirical attitude toward upper-class society in the third novel. *In Their Own Image* presents an even more trenchant judgment of the foibles and immoralities of the idle rich. In fact, the novel depicts a sort of Vanity Fair where all human follies are displayed for the reader's scorn and edification. In this respect the novel is successful, perhaps too much so, for the reader becomes so bored with Basso's shallow parasites that he comes to see the novel itself as dull.

This situation somewhat results from the lack of strong character for reader identification. Pierson James is a well-drawn and sympathetic character, but he remains to a great extent the Jamesian observer or reflector, an experienced, sensitive, intelligent person, but one who does not make things happen. Basso is aware of Pierson's limitations. James is a cripple with a bent neck which gives him a twisted, thwarted look; he was crippled by infantile paralysis when he was in his late thirties, certainly a strange affliction. Yet it has given him an air of false wisdom, as if the twisted angle of his head has provided him an oblique vision different from other men. In order to cultivate his sense of uniqueness he has grown a beard. Basso takes great pains to show us that Pierson is really rather ordinary, a sort of general American personality type—intelligent, hard-working, basically good-hearted. His success in the symbolically American field of advertising is indicative of his typicality. Basso likes the average American, as his book *Mainstream* (1943) clearly demonstrates, and the reader likes Pierson James. At the same time, this character is not capable of dramatizing the indignation which Basso feels, and the reader senses, about the contrasts between the rich and the poor.

For this purpose, the author creates a convenient spokesman in John Pine, a successful painter. Pine's name may be symbolic also, for he towers over the denizens of this phony social world in physical, intellectual, and moral stature. He presents a truly natural point of view which he employs in his art to create a reality not found in the artificial world of the rich. This world includes his dull sister who has married a wealthy banker and invited him to Aiken to do her portrait. Pine is not integral to the plot; he is simply trotted in whenever Basso needs a forceful spokesman for one of his own ideas. However, he does fit into a patterning of characters around the central image pattern drawn from the graphic arts.

For John Pine is not the only artist in Basso's Aiken. Kurt Beach, a young Southerner from Blackwell, Alabama, is an accomplished painter of animal life. In order to support himself in the style to which he would like to become accustomed, Beach gives up his natural bent for Southern subjects and spends his time and talents painting portraits of the Aiken aristocrats' thoroughbred horseflesh. He begins to sell himself out by playing up to his wealthy clients in order to secure commissions; he even makes love to nasty dowagers for this purpose. Pine is visiting Aiken to do a portrait of a wealthy woman, but essentially he keeps himself honest and free, painting his subjects as he sees them and earning just enough to finance his beautiful figure studies. Kurt, by contrast, surrenders his artistic and personal integrity, and he soon loses the ability to do any of his own work.

A third painter is Michael Langford, a millhand from the nearby hamlet of Berrytown, who likes to draw the great mansions of Aiken on his holidays. Michael is the major representative of the milltown plot of the novel, and his artistic honesty also contrasts with Kurt's personal sellout. Not that Michael is a proletarian artist; his friend, Timothy, a labor organizer and strike leader, urges him to use his art as a weapon, but Michael refuses, believing that art is the creation of beauty. He is willing to go out on strike and face the dangers of the picket line, but he will not sacrifice his artistic vision to the cause. His position is, of course, close to the artistic credo which Basso himself was hammering out in the midst of Depression America.

Thus the three graphic artists represent the visions of the three levels of society; Michael's is the sensitive and aspiring vision of the working classes, frustrated by their poverty and ignorance; Kurt's is the corrupt vision of upper classes distorting everything into "their own image"; Pine's is the middle view which clearly sees the rest of society and comments realistically on it. Pine's position is also Basso's, and it is confirmed by the events of the novel.

Most of these events have to do with Kurt's class of people, however. The novel primarily concerns the actions of one social set in Aiken; Michael is depicted only in his visits to Aiken, and Pine is off in his studio most of the time. The greater part of the plot is taken up with the sterile relationships of the upper-class characters. At the center of this group, and providing Pierson James's connection with it, is the Troy family. They made their money in mayonnaise, and the source of their wealth exposes the pretentious absurdity of American class. The Troy fortune was really made by Pierson James's clever, almost artistic, advertising campaigns. After Tom Troy of Rock Center, Illinois, who is reminiscent of Howells's Silas Lapham, established the family business on his wife's old family recipe, James increased it a hundredfold, and the company's workers and managers sustain it. "Good old American know-how," solid as the rock of Rock Center, Illinois, has created Algerlike success. Almost immediately on Tom's death, his widow, Emma, seeks to make the family socially successful also.

Emma marries her son, Freddie, to Benita Sturme (a name Henry James himself would have liked), the wastrel daughter of an old-line New York family which has lost its money in the Crash. Nita is a beautiful but shallow creature who married Freddie for his money and feels free to cuckold him at every opportunity. As the novel opens she is in the middle of an affair with Kurt Beach, an affair which she wants to end. Kurt is helplessly in love with her, and part of his motivation for material success is his hope of holding Nita if he could make his own fortune.

Mrs. Troy is also trying to arrange a marriage between her daughter Virginia and a supercilious Italian nobleman, the Count Piedmontese. Virginia is a level-headed, attractive girl, something of the typical Basso heroine; thus, of course, she resists her mother's pressures. She wants to marry Tom Blackburn, a young architect, with no fortune or family pretensions. The situation is right out of Henry James's international fictions; the pure American girl is threatened by the duplicity of the foreign suitor. The count, of course, is interested only in the family's money and not in Virginia's welfare; in fact he is interested in no one's welfare but his own. He proves to be a selfish phony, who cloaks his self-interest in a philosophical disdain for democratic institutions.

In this respect he becomes a perfect partner for Nita, and the two fortune hunters soon drift together for a brief, boring affair. The other denizens of Aiken are just as self-centered, duplicitous, and ultimately empty people. They include Colonel Thomas, a rather stereotypical British colonial type, a Colonel Blimp who makes another international figure for comparison with the American scene. The colonel is an authority on thoroughbred horses and can say nothing about another subject; Basso seems to imply that he is the final extension of a mindless tradition. He fits in well with the "horsey" members of the Aiken set, especially "Bango" Weems, a polo-playing athlete rather reminiscent of F. Scott Fitzgerald's Tom Buchanan in *The Great Gatsby*. Another athletic type is Herbert Officer, a wealthy banker who fancies himself an expert on boxing and attends the matches in Augusta. Larry Hume is another horseman, but he spends more of his energies on drinking than anything else.

The women in this set include Mrs. Sturme, Nita's widowed mother, who is only slightly less venal than her daughter. Carolyn Grenfell, an attractive middle-aged woman, invariably is mistreated by her lovers and occasionally attempts suicide. "Tippy" McBurnie, a social vulture, is never seen with Mr. McBurnie. Finally, Roberta Smith is another female equivalent of the Count, a tall handsome young woman looking for a fortune to marry. Other women, and men, are occasionally a part of the scene, but the events of the novel revolve about this particular clique.

The novel is divided into five numbered parts, and the first four are centered on the social events of the Aiken aristocracy. When Mr. James arrives at the Troy mansion, he finds the group having preluncheon cocktails. This grouping, with its inevitable inane conversation, serves both to introduce and to type the individuals who make up the group. The gathering is reminiscent of something from Fitzgerald, and Basso maintains just the right level of satirical nastiness. After lunch, the others go off to a polo match, while Mr. James rests in his room. His reminiscences about the Troy family allow Basso to fill in background detail. At the end of the afternoon Mr. James observes Michael Langford sketching the Troy mansion, and decides that the young man is the most interesting person he has seen in Aiken.

Part II introduces the affair between Kurt and Nita, evidently known by everyone in the group, except, of course, Freddie Troy. When Nita finally sends Kurt packing from her bedroom, he also comes upon Michael Langford and his painting. Kurt realizes that Michael represents the urge to art which he once felt, and he envies the younger man his enthusiasm. Michael, for his part, envies what appears to him the easy life of the established artist. At this point Basso sketches in Michael's background, just enough to let the reader understand his symbolic function in the plot. Little of this part of the novel is dramatized, and it certainly doesn't come across as powerfully as the reader might expect. Michael is intelligent enough to make comparisons between the idle lives of the Aiken rich and his own grinding job at the mill; he even makes the comparison of the well-cared-for polo ponies and the poorly fed and housed mill family children. Yet he is too naive and innocent to make this point forcefully. The reader is left with a sense of the conflict, but without a satisfying dramatization of it.

In Part III, John Pine makes many of the same kinds of comparisons, with considerably more force, in his conversations with Mr. James and the other guests at the Aiken houses. A party following the polo match provides another opportunity for the group to reveal their emptiness to both Pine and James. Carolyn Grenfall drunkenly complains about her treatment by Kurt, who has dropped her for Nita; the count has an argument with Bango Weems; and the whole group dissolves into an alcoholic stupor. Later, at a dinner party, Pine has time to expand on his ideas to James. Essentially, he believes that the rich are trying to escape from reality with their money, creating little dream worlds like Aiken and attempting to shut out the real worlds of the cities and the mill villages. The South is particularly fertile soil for such false gardens of Eden because of its unrealistic ancestor-worshiping tradition. His prediction is that the rich are all so useless that they will collapse under the weight of their own ineptitude. Certainly the antics of most of this particular group seem to confirm his theories.

The events of Parts I–III all take place on the day of Pierson James's arrival in Aiken sometime during late February of 1934. Part IV begins about two weeks later, in early March, when the textile strike has just started. Kurt Beach, John Pine, and Mr. James witness a fight between the workers and strikebreakers while they are driving through Berrytown, and the scene is well handled. All the other Aikenites side with the millowners, but these three feel that the workers are taking a reasonable position. A number of arguments ensue, until Mrs. Troy insists that they don't talk "politics" at her dinner party. Sickened by the affair between Nita and the count, Kurt resolves to restore his artistic integrity by going to Berrytown and painting the reality there. But when he makes the trip he finds that the workers reject him as a company spy, and he runs off to sell himself to the rich widow, Mrs. Chisholm, for her portrait commission. Carolyn Grenfell despairs of ever winning him, so she attempts suicide. Nita's affair with the count goes sour, and she blames her mother's secretary, Margaret McGowan, and forces Mrs. Sturme to fire the girl. Most importantly, Michael, idled by the strike, comes back to finish his painting of the Troy house, and he is killed by a security guard who has mistaken him for a burglar.

Part V takes place at the end of March, and it provides a resolution for the complications created in Part IV. Many of the social set have left, fearing a violent reprisal for Michael's death. The count shows his real concerns by leaving Virginia, who is then free to marry Tom Blackburn. Another marriage, more important in a symbolic way, takes place between Mr. James and Mrs. Troy. The implication is clear that Pierson James will be able to restore order in the Troy family. But more disorder proceeds this final reconciliation. Nita precipitates another crisis when she picks up a fighter at one of Mr. Officer's boxing evenings. When she meets him at a hotel in Augusta, Margaret McGowan spies her and calls Freddie, who in turn rushes to Augusta and shoots the boxer. After some trouble he is finally exonerated and begins divorce proceedings against Nita. This sequence takes up most of Part V, and though it is well handled, particularly in long scenes of boxing matches, the whole sequence seems very forced, extraneous, and unmotivated. It is almost as if Basso were looking for some dramatic climax for the novel and seized on the first event to come to mind.

This digression could be forgiven, however, if it were not for the flatness of the rest of Basso's resolution of plot complications. Basso has everyone married and living happily ever after. The Troy family is redeemed by going back to sensible middle-class virtues. Yet this reconciliation seems too facile, rather like the conclusion of many a 1930s film comedy where the social-climbing wife receives her comeuppance and realizes the error of her ways. Thus Pierson James becomes a sort of a cross between Lambert Strether and Will Rogers. This ending might do for a musical comedy, but it is too facile for the tragic implications of the textile strike plot. Basso appears to beg the questions of social inequity and economic inequality which his spokesman, John Pine, eloquently raises in the novel.

Yet the novelist must be given credit for raising these issues. Clearly Basso's heart is on the right side, the side of the underdog, in the industrial struggles of the Depression. His several journalistic pieces on Southern textile strikes incisively analyze the causes and effects of industrial warfare. The reader taking time to contrast this nonfiction reporting with the novel is struck by the greater force of the former. Basso has simply not been able to get inside his working-class characters. They remain unsubstantial and unconvincing, and he is unable even to integrate them symbolically into his novel's plot. Michael's death is the dramatic climax of the novel, but it is not resolved by the conclusion of the novel. The fear, hatred, and guilt created by this near murder are not resolved but simply forgotten as the novel moves off to Nita's bizarre infatuation and the perfunctory pairing of the other characters in marriage. His ending, very simply put, does not work.

What does work is his realistic picturing of the effete, snobbish world of Aiken. His characterizations are incisive, his dialogue is accurate, his events (at least in Parts I-III) are believable. These minor characters and scenes are as good as much of Fitzgerald or Sinclair Lewis, or of Henry James, for that matter. The early part of the novel works well as a realistic indictment of America's corrupt wealth. The ideas about the suffering poor are also liberal, though not as well dramatized. Most importantly, the novel lacks a solid conclusion, and a solid character for reader identification. In his next novel, *Courthouse Square*, Basso returns to his more typical protagonist, a young Southern novelist trying to go home again to South Carolina, and in this more carefully plotted novel he presents a successful portrait of the South in the throes of the Depression.

III   Courthouse Square

Reviewing *Courthouse Square* in the *New York Herald Tribune* for november 1, 1936, the novelist Lyle Saxon wrote, "This is Hamilton Basso's best novel to date; it places him among the significant writers of the South, and it is a fine fulfillment of the promise given in his earlier books."[2] Such high praise was echoed in other reviews, and *Courthouse Square* established Basso as a young South writer of some importance, one to be compared with Wolfe, Faulkner, and Caldwell. Saxon's judgment is incisive as well as laudatory because he sees the novel as a natural development of Basso's talents and achievements. In a sense, *Courthouse Square* combines the best elements of his

three previous books, creating, perhaps, his most fully representative novel.

In *Courthouse Square* Basso returned to the autobiographical
character found most often at the center of his novels. In fact,
David Barondess, the protagonist of this book, is not merely
another sensitive young Southerner, he is a Southern writer who
has published two novels critical of the South. Unlike the earlier
autobiographical heroes, Tony Clezac and Dekker Blackheath,
who were both born in New Orleans, David is a South Carolinian, but like Basso he was educated in New Orleans and
worked there as a newspaper reporter before leaving for New
York and literary success. The novel is set in the present (1936),
and David is about the same age as his creator, thirty-one or
thirty-two. There are a few flashbacks to his youth, but for the
most part David's boyhood, and even young manhood, are not at
issue here. Instead, the novel relies more on Basso's later life for
its inspiration, particularly his social observations in South
Carolina which were also used for *In Their Own Image.*

David is a more mature and effective character than the
earlier variations of Basso's autobiographical protagonists. He is
older, more talented, and more successful; at the same time he
remains gentle, sensitive, and rather confused. His confusion,
again like the earlier protagonists, exists essentially in terms of
his relationship with his past as part of a region, a town, and a
family. David Barondess is forced to return home in an attempt
to find himself in the Southern roots of his experience. The
journey into his own past, his personal heart of darkness, nearly
destroys him, though he does escape at last with a real
knowledge which augurs well for his future as a man and as an
artist.

David's past is Macedon, South Carolina, a typical Southern
county seat and market town. As usual, names are significant for
Basso. Macedon sits among the Piedmont hills, and, like its
ancient namesake, it is a half civilized place which has produced
a hearty race of warriors. The place and the people were
corrupted by the vice of slavery, however, and instead of
expanding to the world Macedon turned in on itself after the
Civil War. Its paramount characteristic is stasis; nothing changes,
David discovers after a decade's absence; indeed nothing has
changed since the Civil War. Nothing could change because the

town, like the larger South which it represents, had to cling to its false vision of itself in order to justify the economic exploitation which was its real identity.

In researching his grandfather's life for a biography, David discovers this thesis and succinctly states it in his notes.

And all the while, really, they were ashamed of slavery. Even a man like Jefferson Davis, in that cold arrogant soul of his, was secretly ashamed of it. Yet, believing that the end of slavery meant the end of the South, a general collapse of all property values and subsequent ruin—and God knows it did!—and being constantly harried by the rabid Abolitionists (who were financed, interestingly enough, largely by the Yankee industrialists) they were finally driven into sublimating the rank injustice of slavery into one of the greatest humanitarian movements of all times. Nor is this to be wondered at. History is full of such sublimations. It is one of the things that happen when two different orders collide. (84)

The South and Macedon had to fight a bloody, hopeless war in defense of that sublimation. After their inevitable defeat, they constructed alternate social systems, like sharecropping, along with new sublimations to justify them. David later notes:

What looks like decay in the South—tenant farming, for example—is, most often, simply the result of an abortive effort to maintain the culture of 1860 on the economic foundation, and in the changed moral climate of today. (200)

These corrupt systems and systematic corruptions have been passed down to the present generation, forming them in the image of the past. Yet the people of the present cannot simply excuse themselves by an appeal to historical necessity, as David tells his Southern friends.

Those of us who live here today are being held responsible for history—for things that began a hundred years ago. We didn't invent tenant farming. We didn't start racial discrimination. We didn't lure mountaineers out of the hills and herd them in mill villages. We can shove all that off on our fathers and grandfathers—and even bring in climate, geography and technology to help shoulder the blame. But, nevertheless, tenant farming, racial discrimination and mill villages *are* our responsibility. The only honorable thing we can do, it seems to me, is to accept that responsibility. I once wrote that it was part of our heritage. (155)

Thus the sensitive young Southerner, including David Barondess and Basso's other protagonists, must wander like Ulysses,
ever seeking new vistas, but ever turning homeward again to
some dark Ithaca. Since David is a novelist, he can discuss this
Ulysses theme in a literary context, mentioning his fellow
Southern writers B. F. (Bill Faulkner) and T. W. (Thomas Wolfe).

. . . I remembered how B. F. used to spend hours talking about
home; not liking it at all, feeling that he was not respected or trusted,
and yet, in an interesting and curious way, pulled back to it emotionally.
(200)

o o o o o

It may be said that T. W.'s many paged wandering is also religious:
the father idea equalling the God idea. (201)

All the young men created by these writers wander the world in
search of a father figure; when they don't find one, they must
return home again to establish their real identities. Their
heritage includes moonlight and magnolias, Jim Crow laws and
mill villages; their forebears include dashing cavalrymen and
foolish weaklings destroyed by their circumstances. Faulkner's
Quentin Compson and Wolfe's Eugene Gant could be compared
with Basso's earlier protagonists; David Barondess is more akin
to Ike McCaslin and Monk Webber, stronger young men trying to
define themselves in relation to society and history.

The success of *Courthouse Square* is not in the evocation of
social and historical themes; rather, as in the works of Faulkner
and Wolfe, it lies in the successful integration of theme with
narrative. Basso discovers in the history of the Barondess family a
story which crystalizes the meaning of Southern history as aptly
as Faulkner's complicated genealogies; in the person of David
Barondess the author creates a character as capable of knowing
the contemporary world as Wolfe's wanderers. Not that plotting
is perfect; there are some superfluous characters, muddy
motivations, and a few loose ends. Yet more than in any of his
other novels Basso integrates this story with his ideas. Using the
character of a writer as protagonist allows him to editorialize a
bit, as in the passages quoted above, but these preachings are
well integrated into a narrative which aptly demonstrates their
essential accuracy.

Macedon was founded in the eighteenth century by the
Legendre family, who dominated the cotton-growing community

through the period of the Civil War and built the great house of
the area on the first hill outside of the town. Macedon's principal
hero in that conflict was Cincinnatus Quintius Legendre, suitably
immortalized in bronze in the middle of the courthouse square.
Basso's description of the statue nicely plays on the ironic
relationship of past to present.

He stands with one foot forward, the metal folds of his cloak swirling as
in a storm, brooding with fixed and rigid eyes, and gray, as from the dust
of a long campaign, with the accumulated droppings of many birds. (3)

Old Cincinnatus was the last of the legendary Legendres; after
the Civil War the family name disappears (like Faulkner's
Sutpens) as the only daughter marries into the less noble Lamar
family. Even the Lamars soon abandon the Legendre Mansion,
and this old ruin becomes symbolic of the ruined older order.

Some of Macedon's citizens could see the seeds of ruin in the
sins of that exploitive order. Edward Barondess, David's
grandfather, was also a successful cotton planter who built a big
house, though not a grand one, on the next ridge past the
Legendre mansion. Their name seems to indicate the true
nobility of the Barondess family. Edward seriously questioned
both the economic and moral viability of slavery, and, like many
Southerners of conscience, he worked for gradual, voluntary
emancipation. Unlike most, he felt strongly enough about the
ultimate justice of this cause to abandon the South to hotheads
like Legendre and St. John Lamar while he went off to fight in
the Union army. From this day his home became the Jayhawker
House, and its setting, Abolitionist Hill. Yet Edward returned
from the war and attempted to work out a just sharecropping
system for the liberated slaves. He was unsuccessful, and the
family fortunes went into decline.

Fortunately, his son, John Barondess, was intelligent enough to
win a scholarship to Harvard Law School and hardworking
enough to gain the local judgeship in spite of the family name.
John soon clashed with the system of Jim Crow justice much as
his father had opposed slavery. A black gambler named "Frog
Eye" Jones is convicted of murder by public prosecutor Toomer
Lamar, but John suspects that the testimony of the state's chief
witness is perjured, and so reverses the decision. He is voted out
in the next election, and Toomer Lamar is voted in. His legal

career is ruined, of course, but like his father he refuses to move away and courageously continues to fight for racial justice. The death of his wife, Marie, a Creole beauty from New Orleans, leaves him completely despondent, and he gives up even his intellectual life. The family seems destined for complete ruin until his sister, Celia, marries Lucius Hempstead, a solid, "downhome" cotton factor, who restores some order on Abolitionist Hill.

David's mother had died when he was about twelve, and he grew up with Aunt Celia and Uncle "Loosh" as surrogate parents. His father retreated farther into himself until he was only a ruined shell of his former self, rather like a decaying old house. His father's distance and ineffectuality infuriated young David, who felt compelled to leave Macedon and find his true home and father somewhere else.

He goes to college in New Orleans, and works there on a newspaper, until making the young writer's ambitious trek to New York. There he becomes part of a typical Bohemian group and produces a first novel, which is ignored by the critics. He meets and marries Letitia Graham, a Maryland girl, who has been educated in Anthropology at Columbia. His second novel is a critical and financial success, but his life and his love are failures.

His moment of crisis comes when his wife becomes pregnant. Soon he will have to adopt the archetypal father's role, which his father has been so unsuccessful in. David reverts to adolescence and is unfaithful to his wife; she loses the baby and leaves him. At this juncture he knows that he must come home again to define himself before he can achieve his maturity in his personal life or his literary career.

The narrative opens at this point, with David returned home to Macedon in March of 1936, standing in the courthouse square and contemplating the changeless face of the town. He visits the drugstore for a pack of cigarettes and finds one small change—a soda fountain has been installed. But "Doc" Murphy, the town pharmacist, has not changed at all in the decade David has been gone; he soon fills the prodigal in on the town's gossip. David's return to Abolitionist Hill is also pleasant; the fatted calf (or in this case, a lamb) is presented, and everyone, even his estranged father, seems happy to see him home, at least until he reveals that his wife has left him; the family has never had a divorce, and

Aunt Celia does not want to see one now. Later, Pick Eustis, the literarily ambitious editor of the *Macedon Mercury*, writes an editorial welcoming the young wanderer back to town, much like ones that appeared in the Asheville paper when Wolfe finally made his peace with his homeplace. David's first day in Macedon tricks him into thinking that he can go home again.

Into a Southern April that "drowsed and daydreamed . . . like a girl in love" (83), David works at finding his place in Macedon and the South. His literary work now is a biography of his grandfather, Edward Barondess, the Southern Abolitionist. Reading over the old letters and journals, David's vision of Southern history begins to form, much as outlined above. At the same time he takes up with his old friends to regain his personal life, particularly with Phil Leslie, a young doctor who had been at college with him. Playing tennis with Phil he meets Julie Lamar, an old girl friend, who is now married to Toomer Lamar's son, Dan, a Snopesian garage owner. He also flirts innocently with Melissa King, a teenager who has always had a crush on him. These flirtations, though Julie Lamar is soon flirting less innocently with him, are signs of his continued adolescence, his inability to accept his mature role and get back together with his wife. His lack of artistic maturity is evident in his inability to actually start writing the biography; all he can do is make notes like a high-school student on a library project.

In late April events begins shaping themselves into a pattern of confrontation which will become the catalyst of David's maturation. Doc Murphy is not the town's only druggist; on the other side of the tracks a pharmacy for blacks is run by Alcide Fauget, a tiny old man who looks almost white. Fauget had achieved some fame in the town by performing an emergency tracheotomy on a young girl in the local café, and he is respected by both the black and white communities. It is revealed later than Fauget is the illegitimate son of Cincinnatus Legendre and an octoroon woman of New Orleans. He was raised by his mother in comfortable circumstances and was able to "pass" well enough to be admitted to a white medical school. After his graduation, he refused to continue in this false identity and returned to help his people as a doctor. When he married he returned to Macedon, where he opened the pharmacy and did not practice medicine openly for fear of revealing his identity. His wife is now dead and Fauget, feeling that he too is approaching death, decides to benefit his people with the profits from the pharmacy.

He plans to buy the old Legendre Mansion and turn it into a hospital for blacks, as they are refused treatment at Macedon's white hospital.

Fauget contacts John Barondess, his lawyer, to effect the sale. When news of Fauget's intentions are rumored about the town, the white community reacts with alarm at the symbolism of transforming a great "white" house, though fallen in ruins, into a black hospital. White resentment turns not so much against Fauget as John Barondess, who is accused of encouraging the black pharmacist in much the same manner in which he crossed the community in the case of "Frog Eye" Jones. Pick Eustis writes a scathing editorial attacking Fauget and the Barondess family; Swinton Buttonwood, the local pettifogging lawyer, seeks some legal red tape to prevent the sale; and Dan Lamar excites the rednecks toward a violent resolution.

Lamar is motivated by more than Southern chauvinism, as he has always disliked David and now is jealous of his wife's interest in the writer. His personal hysteria is increased when he drunkenly accuses his wife of adultery, and she walks out on him. Lamar's situation now parallels David's and he reacts even more adolescently by seeking a violent confrontation with his antagonist. David, of course, supports the Fauget project and his father's connection with it, so he refuses to run from a fight. Lamar avoids a direct attack on David by leading a lynch mob after Fauget; David hears of his intention and, with Phil Leslie, manages to rescue Fauget from the mob. During the rescue David is hit by a brick and then badly beaten by Lamar and his cronies before Loosh and the sheriff can rescue him. As a result of the riot both Fauget's pharmacy and the Legendre house are burned to the ground.

The symbolism here is somewhat obvious but still effective. The traditions of the old South which support the modern community of Macedon are for the most part inoperative old legends. The Legendre house and the values it represents are useless to the people of Macedon, both black and white. When any progressive measure, such as Fauget's hospital plan, is proposed, the fearful reaction of the conservative majority destroys even the little good within the old tradition. Thus the events of the novel neatly dramatize the themes which Basso articulates through David's diary entries. And if David's vision is not clearly enough articulated, Basso adds John Barondess's interior voice to the argument:

It was the South again, the history and psychology of the South, the old incubus of slavery yet lying across the land—punishment for the sins of the fathers being imposed even unto the third and fourth generation. It was the shame of the Old South (for it was ashamed of slavery—all its sophistry and protesting rhetoric stemmed from shame) transmuted into the defiance and resentment and prejudice of the new. It was isolation, the distrust of strangers and new ideas and outside things. It was the character of a section, its social structure, influencing the character of man. (43)

Almost the entire portion of the book dealing with Macedon is effectively handled in terms of theme, symbolism, and even narrative details. The Southern characters are all well drawn and completely believable. David's family is reminiscent of Dekker Blackwood's in *Cinnamon Seed;* in particular, Aunt Celia is another lively version of the Southern gentlewoman portrayed by Aunt Olivia in the earlier novel. Uncle Loosh provides a sprightly mate for her, with his addiction to tall stories, practical jokes, and radio serials. John Barondess is somewhat less palpable, but this is understandable given his defeated position at the time of the narrative. The other white townsfolk from Phil Leslie, the liberal doctor, to Dan Lamar, the racist garage owner, are all nearly perfectly done, as are the minor characters, such as the hateful Pick Eustis, the adenodial "soda jerk" in the pharmacy, the members of Mrs. Buttonwood's bridge club, and Kolopoxos, the owner of the Dixie-American Restaurant. Several times Basso switches from immediate observation of his central character to sections called "The Voices of the Town" which demonstrate the reactions of minor characters who combine as a sort of commenting chorus. The overall effect of these sections is to produce a sense of the whole town, a whole milieu, perfectly recreated in a novel, something Basso would do on a much larger scale in the Pompey's Head novels.

Within this scheme, the black characters are something of a problem, as in *Cinnamon Seed.* Fauget is one of Basso's most memorable creations, a characterization even Faulkner could be proud of. Yet it must be remembered that Fauget is fifteen-sixteenths white, so that even his Christlike identification with the downtrodden blacks is only a slight extension of the Barondess's liberal positions on racial issues. The real blacks are believable, but again slightly stereotyped. Emmy, the family cook, is a bit too much in the Aunt Jemima mold; and her husband, Hamburg, recalls Horace from *Cinamon Seed*. Hamburg and his brother-in-law Jim do several "Amos and Andy" routines that are made even more problematic by Basso's heavy use of dialect spelling. Other than the near-white Fauget, none of the blacks has an important role in the novel, a situation which increasingly obtains in Basso's books. Unfortunately, as minor characters, his blacks tend toward local color and comedy relief.

These problems do not seriously mar the realistic portrait of the South presented in the Macedon sections. Much more of a difficulty for the overall novel is created by the New York sections. At least a third of the book concerns David's life in New York, all of it presented through reminiscent flashback. This technique is rather obvious and intrusive as Basso had not learned to handle the device as aptly as he does in later novels. The material proves even more problematic than the technique, as these flashbacks almost wholly concern his marriage and his literary career—two areas which were perennially difficult for Basso's fictions. As usual, his wife, Letitia, is rather unsubstantial and unbelievable as a characterization; while his literary buddies, Jack, Thad, and Pete, are right out of a third-rate movie. Basso does manage to convey the suffocating phoniness of a New York literary party, yet, as in the social gatherings at Aiken in his previous novel, he succeeds at the cost of boring the reader. Some small details of the New York scene—a Village restaurant, a Westside apartment, a walk in the park—are well done but rather superfluous to the novel as a whole.

The major difficulty, however, is David's relationship with Letitia. From the beginning it seems rather unmotivated and overly romantic. Its crisis is David's infidelity with a beautiful movie starlet and Letitia's resulting loss of her unborn baby. And its resolution occurs when Letitia not only forgives him but accepts the blame for the failure and recognizes what a completely admirable character David really is. This, to put it simply, does not make human sense. Letitia at least has more force than the typical Basso heroine: she is occasionally less than sweet, genteel, and well dressed; she even worries about her own needs and career. Yet at the crunch all this goes out the window. David undoubtedly has matured through his suffering and does deserve forgiveness so that he can begin his mature careers as husband and artist, but the manner of the resolution smacks too much of the woman's novel or movie solution of the period—the wife will nobly sacrifice herself in order to support her noble husband.

These problems of occasional failures of Realism, unconvincing female characters and commercial endings, were seen in Basso's earlier novels, and they will continue to exist in his later books. However, they do not cancel out the very real achievements of these works in their realistic portrayal of the tragedy of history working itself out in the modern South. Basso's next pair of novels will put more emphasis on modern as against Southern history, and they mark a new maturity of his artistic vision.

CHAPTER 4

The Philosophical Novels

I Days Before Lent

C OURTHOUSE Square (1936) established Hamilton Basso's reputation as a young Southern novelist of considerable sensitivity and skill; *Days Before Lent* (1939) confirmed that well-deserved reputation. The new book was both a critical and a popular success; it won the Southern Authors Award for 1940, and it was eventually sold to the movies. Like *Courthouse Square, Days Before Lent* combines several elements of earlier novels, elements which are always strong points in Basso's fiction. The protagonist, Dr. Jason Kent, is a particularly engaging version of the Basso hero. The plot unfolds with a good deal of romance and violence in the colorful setting of New Orleans on the eve of Mardi Gras. Obviously, these elements accounted for the book's popular success. Its critical success rested on an appreciation of stylistic achievement, artistic integrity, and realistic intelligence. Alfred Kazin, reviewing the novel for the *New York Times,* compared it with the work of Wolfe and Faulkner, seeing it as evidence of a new and intelligent Realism taking root in the South.[1] Kazin and other reviewers attested to the novel's serious portrayal of important contemporary problems and ideas. *Days Before Lent* proves a very fine novel in its combination of Basso's realistic fictional strengths with a new complexity of idea and theme.

Basso's previous three novels had all been strengthened by a realistic sense of social problems and possible solutions; these issues, however, were confined mainly to the South and worked out in Southern terms. Although *Days Before Lent,* and Basso's next two novels— *Wine of the Country* (1941) and *Sun In Capricorn* (1942)—concern Southern protagonists and are set in the South (at least partially), they use the Southern experience metaphorically to depict an even broader spectrum of human experience. Basso's expanded vision could be explained at least in part by the difference of the news he reported for the *New Republic* over these years. His emphasis changed from national to international events; the Depression still plagued the United States, but after the presidential election of 1936 domestic events took less of the liberal's concern than ominous developments in Europe and Asia. Basso traveled in Europe in 1938, and he was keenly aware of the portents involved in the militaristic posturings of Fascist and Communist dictators. Like many sensitive minds of the day, Basso began to fear the possible extinction of civilization.

During this period Basso returned to his earlier interests, science and anthropology, in a search for universal truths about man and his condition. Naturally enough his fiction soon began to reflect these wider concerns; his protagonists are now doctors and anthropologists rather than novelists and advertising men. But it is in theme, not just subject matter, that the most important changes take place. In one sense *Days Before Lent* is another story of the sensitive young Southerner coming to terms with himself and his past; in another it is a parable of the condition of humankind faced with the real possibility of annihilation. From its multiple epigraphs to its concluding chapter the novel attempts to demonstrate the unity of human experience within the life of the physical universe. The story of Jason Kent dramatizes the necessity not just of recognizing this unity but of acting from this knowledge to a purposeful, humanistic life-style.

In this thematic aspect there is much which seems very contemporary about the novel. Environmentalism, preventive medicine, and structural anthropology are all anticipated in the concerns of Basso's intellectual characters. Jason's father, Peter Kent, was both a medical doctor who preached the gospel of preventive medicine and an impassioned amateur anthropologist who recognized the connections between religion and medicine. His friend Dr. Gomez, an exiled revolutionary from a Central American "banana" republic, insisted on the continuity between man and nature, fearing that as man becomes overly civilized he loses something of his essential human nature. Jason's surrogate father figure, Dr. Jonathon Hunt, an eminent bacteriologist, is also something of a philosopher, who strives to connect biology with psychology. Father Victor Carducci, a longtime friend of

Jason's, agonizes about the balance between the spiritual life and the material life, not wishing to preach pie in the sky to his Depression-stricken parishioners. All of these men portray the struggles for unity of human response which Jason himself must discover in the course of the novel, and all of these struggles have become even more important a generation after the publication of *Days Before Lent.*

As usual in a Basso novel, the thematic import is centered in the emergence of the protagonist, in this case Dr. Jason Kent, M.D. Jason is another variation of the autobiographical persona seen in Tony Clezac, Dekker Blackheath, and David Barondess. Like these others, he has a symbolic name, given him by his father, who wishes the boy to be a seeker after the golden fleece, the symbolic treasure of personal integrity and fulfillment. Jason has sought this personal integration in religion, in science, and in the humanities at various stages of his life. He was born and raised in the French Quarter of New Orleans, educated locally, sojourned briefly in New York, and now has returned again to become engaged to a beautiful visitor from New England, Susanna Fuller. The resemblances to Tony, Dekker, and Basso himself are many and obvious, and, as in Basso's first two novels, the reminiscence of a New Orleans boyhood, with visits to the back bayous, are used to the advantage of local color.

Even more color is derived from the present setting, New Orleans in the late 1930s during Mardi Gras Week. Basso begins his book at the first stirrings of the carnival and ends it at the climax of Mardi Gras itself. The strange combination of bacchanal, country-club dance, and tourist promotion, which is the modern Mardi Gras celebration, provides not only a colorful setting but a symbolic one as well. The celebration is a sort of mindless Vanity Fair, a time of tinsel and pretense, a temporary sensual diversion from the responsibilities of living, which extends to the local rich, the middle-class tourists, and the proletarians of New Orleans. None of the novel's major characters really partakes of the festival; they all see it as at best a nuisance, at worst a symbol of what modern society has become, a place of senseless illusion in the face of destruction. Surely these days before Lent have lost their religious significance, for no penance will follow the debauch; after the knowledge of modern life there can be no forgiveness.

Jason is possessed of the full knowledge of modern life. Like the other Basso protagonists, he is a sensitive and intelligent man, quick to see and understand the world around him. Even more than the others, he proves to be a very pragmatic person who does not wish to waste his life on romantic gestures. Instead, he searches through his education for a practical path to meaningful action. As the novel opens he is thirty, at the point where he must choose his true path of development. He is helped in this regard by a fine general education; a number of father figures have given him his emotional education, while the university has provided a strict, intellectual training in his specialty, bacteriology. Now he is faced by the problem of how to utilize his talents. Should he devote himself to pure science, becoming a sort of priest of medicine, by going off to India with Dr. Hunt, who is going to continue his researches into the communicable diseases? Should he use his general medical skills to help the poor people of New Orleans, as his father has done before him? Or should he take a sinecure with a large corporation which he has been offered through his social connections? Aside from these choices he must decide how Susanna will fit into his vocational plans.

The novel essentially works out Jason's solution to these problems by bringing him into contact with a number of symbolic figures who represent various choices of belief and life-style. First there are the father figures: Peter Kent and Father John, the bayou priest, both now dead and presented only in flashback and reminiscence. Next are the surrogate fathers: Dr. Gomez, Dr. Hunt, and Dr. Ernst Muller, head of the local health service. Next there are the young men who serve as foils for Jason: Joe Piavi, a broken-down boxer who had once been a protégé of Peter Kent's; Danny O'Neill, a cousin on Jason's mother's side, who is a tough-guy police reporter; Tyrell Surtees, a cousin on his father's side, a sort of Tennessee Williams version of a decadent Southern playwright; and Father Victor, who has grown up with Jason and who is more brother than father to him. There are many other characters in this large, panoramic novel, but only one is of importance, Susanna, the fiancée and the only woman of any importance in the book. Unfortunately, as in the earlier novels, her portrait is more caricature than characterization, and Miss Fuller is as thoroughly unbelievable as any woman's book heroine of the period. Fortunately her role is more symbolic than not, and her portrayal does not significantly weaken the novel.

The novel opens on the Thursday before Mardi Gras with Jason alone in his apartment trying to complete a scientific treatise on *Kala-azar,* a tropical disease which he has encountered and fought in the bayous of Louisiana; in its detailed depiction of medical research and an idealistic young doctor, the book recalls Sincair Lewis's *Arrowsmith* (1925). About three years before the present of the novel Jason had been vacationing in the back bayous with Fr. Victor as a companion. The priest's uncle, Fr. John, had told them about a strange malady which was afflicting his Cajun parishioners. At first, Jason was unable to diagnose the disease, but a chance meeting with two Chinese fishermen gave him the clue he needed. *Kala-azar* is an Asiatic disease carried into the region with smuggled Chinese refugees. He also remembered a treatment suggested by Dr. Hunt in one of his university lectures—the use of intravenous antimony tartrate. However, he didn't remember the correct dosage and his first experiments killed several of his patients, including Fr. John. His quick action finally did prevent the spread of the plague, and Dr. Muller was able to come down from New Orleans and mop up after Jason himself collapsed. The affair made him something of a medical hero, and led to both the offer from Dr. Hunt to be his assistant and the offer from a large corporation to head its research department.

At the beginning of the novel Jason is struggling to complete his treatise, but he is impeded more by his personal tensions than by the difficulties of subject matter. He knows all there is to know about the parasites of *Kala-azar;* he must learn more about the human equations which have affected his own life because of the epidemic three years earlier. As he wonders about his future he recalls his conversation with Dr. Hunt and Dr. Muller the night before and their insistence that he take the position with Hunt in India. Both men are surrogate fathers, and both represent his formal education and his dedication to science. But there is a crucial difference between them.

And yet, despite the mental boot-heel clicking, he liked and respected Muller enormously. One had to admit his thoroughness, his relentless oxlike driving; and in the laboratory there was something almost beautiful about the sureness and precision with which he worked. His technic, actually, was better than the Old Man's—though he would never have Hunt's delicacy and grace. Watching the Old Man was like watching an artist. Muller was science through and through. And there was a time, Jason remembered, when he thanked God that he was. If it hadn't been for Muller in the bayou country—Good Ernie, really. (9)

Jason respects Muller, but he admires Hunt. Jason's direction is toward the artistic, humanistic side of science, not toward the Prussian precision of a Muller. Hunt represents the real pull of science for him, but even this is a cold, abstract science which looks at bacteria, not at people. Thus for Jason it is not Hunt or Muller, but:

Hunt or Susanna? Susanna or Hunt? To keep the one, he must reject the other. No compromise was possible. Which to keep, which to reject, he did not know. (23)

This is the equation which he must solve in the course of the novel.

Since he can come to no easy conclusion, he throws up his work and breaks for lunch, but before he can leave a visitor arrives, Joe Piavi, the broken-down prize fighter. Jason has taken over Joe's case after his father's death. Peter Kent had been an amateur boxer himself, and his cultivation of Joe was a sort of indulgence of his own tough side, his animal nature. Jason had boxing lessons, but had never taken to the sport; so that Joe is a kind of dark, violent brother, an extension of the material man inside the spiritual man. (More than a little resemblance exists between the pug and Jason's pet monkey, Bobo.) Jason tries to guide Joe, but he fails as Joe sinks deeper into a dark pit of booze, drugs, and petty crime. Joe's accelerating decline will provide the melodramatic action of the novel's conclusion.

Another foil for Jason, who also represents the darker possibilities of man's nature, is his cousin Danny O'Neill. Danny is just Jason's age though he looks five or six years older. He has been precocious in corruption, giving himself over to drinking and philandering in the French Quarter while following the local criminal element as a police reporter. After Joe leaves, Jason visits Danny's apartment and finds him just emerging from a hangover. Later they go to lunch at a newspaper hangout where they meet two more cynical "gentlemen of the press," Rogers and Price. Their conversation dwells on the latest gangland murder and the arrival for Mardi Gras of Jason's other cousin, Tyrell Surtees, the decadent playwright.

After lunch Jason walks back across Jackson Square to visit his friend Fr. Victor at the Cathedral Chapel. As in Basso's first novel, *Relics and Angels*, the geographical setting takes on symbolic overtones. From the world of science, and the world of shabby politics and crime, Jason returns to the order of religion; he even thinks about going into the cathedral to pray. But he cannot go home again to his lost faith, and when he arrives at the rectory Fr. Victor is out. Jason then wanders down to the river to walk the docks and contemplate his personal decisions.

In the evening he goes to dinner with Dr. Gomez, his father's old friend who has taken over his practice after his death. Gomez is both a philosopher and a man of action; he has been expelled from his own country by the military dictatorship, and he longs to return and restore democracy. But the years have weakened this resolve as they have also strengthened the dictator's iron grip on the Central American land. Now almost seventy, Gomez is bitter about the decline of Europe into Fascism, and the facile belief that science alone can save man.

It is blind! What stupid folly to talk of conquering the earth! It is not the earth that is being conquered. It is man. Do they not realize that? Do they not understand that as man subdues nature he subdues himself—that man, being an animal, is as dependent upon the operation of natural laws as an amoeba or a frog? Isn't it possible for them to get into their over-educated heads that the mechanized culture of modern society has almost destroyed a relationship that is vitually essential to man—not for any sentimental or mystical reasons, but biological ones! They claim to think scientifically. What a farce! They talk about thinking scientifically and yet they fail to understand the simple scientific fact that certain balances cannot be destroyed without destroying a species. (169)

The old doctor sees the decline of democracy as symptomatic of the failure of science to educate men to true freedom. Jason agrees with him, but he can see no better way to handle the modern world than through scientific advances.

After leaving Dr. Gomez, Jason wanders the mean streets of New Orleans looking for Joe Piavi, trying to prevent him from getting into real trouble. At a poolroom he finds out that Joe has

threatened a local gangster, Nick Weinstein. Late that night he
stays at the French market for late coffee and meets Tyrell
Surtees with several of his socialite friends, who then invite him
to a late-night party. Here he has a chance to talk with Tyrell,
who has lapsed into despondency because of his wife's suicide
several months earlier. If his cousin Danny represents what the
unbridled physical nature can be, Tyrell symbolizes the
unchecked intellect. He is all mind and all nerves, a neurasthenic
consciousness with all the neuroses of the modern world. Jason
stays as long as he can stand Tyrell's pseudosophisticated
companions, first cousins to the idle rich of Aiken from *In Their
Own Image*, and then wanders home to bed.

The actions of this first day involve, with long flashbacks to
previous action, over half the novel: setting up the major
problems, introducing the major characters, and presenting the
important symbols which will be drawn together in the book's
resolution. The novel then jumps from Thursday to Sunday, the
day of Susanna's arrival and clearly a moment of crisis for Jason.
Again Jason sits at his desk, trying to work on his treatise; again
he is frustrated, gives up, and walks the streets of the Quarter in
his restlessness. On his return he meets Father Victor at his
apartment. The priest is the antithesis of his latest visitor, Joe
Piavi, in almost every respect. He represents the spiritual
element of man drawn out to its fullest extent. Like Joe, Victor is
in personal difficulty, and he needs Jason's help almost as much.
Fr. Victor has devised a plan to help the poor of the district by
taking over a large, abandoned warehouse near the river and
transforming it into a communal home for the poor. The
symbolism here is reminiscent of *Courthouse Square* and Dr.
Fauget's plans for the Negro Hospital. Fr. Victor, like Fauget, is
frustrated by the forces of social inertia; the conservative Bishop
of New Orleans fears that the cooperative might seem commu-
nistic, and he orders the priest to drop the plan. Fr. Victor knows
that his project is the truly Christian thing to do in these
circumstances, and he is faced with the dilemma of acting as a
Christian and being expelled from the Church, or staying in the
Church and abandoning his Christian ideas. Caught up in Victor's
crisis, Jason decides to let other friends meet Susanna at the
railroad station, thus postponing his own decision about a
vocation.

The next day, Monday, he calls her for lunch, but she is out sightseeing with her hostess. Instead, Jason lunches with Dr. Gomez and receives another jolt which affects his own plans. The old man is going back to his country to make one last attempt at revolution, and he offers Jason his practice. Suddenly Jason has another alternative which had not occurred to him earlier. In the course of their conversation Gomez warns Jason about giving too much weight to abstract principle, in effect telling him to think twice about going to India.

Were it not for these men of "principle," these fanatics with fixed and rigid minds, Communists, Fascists, Papists, all these absolutists, predeterminists, fatalists—were it not for such men of "principle," all of them at each other's "principled" throats, we would not have all this claptrap of high-sounding slogans. "Principles," in this wretched time, have become nothing but emotional symbols of partisanship. If it were not for these symbols—if we had fewer "principles" and more morality in the world—men might be able to think true. There might be a chance for a little more tolerance and humanity on the earth. (237)

Jason begins to see the rightness of the old man's position; perhaps humanism offers alternatives to science.

Monday evening is the traditional night of the great masked balls which usher in Mardi Gras proper, and Jason is to meet Susanna at the largest of them, the Masque of Proteus. On the way to the ball Jason stops to buy a newspaper and discovers that Nick Weinstein has been murdered. He realizes at once that Joe has made good his crazy threat and that he must find him before Weinstein's gangsters can avenge their boss's death. Again he abandons Susanna and sets off on a nightmarish search through the dark streets filled with masked revelers. This is the real meaning of the carnival: the mad violence of the streets, not the pleasantries of the ball.

Mardi Gras, Tuesday, resolves all of these lines of development. Jason goes back to his apartment for a few hours' sleep and then races out again after Joe. In the meantime Joe comes back to the apartment looking for another loan and meets Danny O'Neill, who is there for the same purpose. Danny, sensing a great story, talks Joe into surrendering at the newspaper office for his own protection. But when they try to walk through the thronged streets of the Quarter, Weinstein's gunmen spot them and shoot both of them down. Thus the unbridled animal nature of man dies in its own image of violence, just as Joe had killed Jason's pet monkey a few minutes earlier in a fit of fear and anger. The unbridled intellect also meets a violent end. Tyrell Surtees, haunted by the specter of his betrayed wife, follows her in suicide, flying his airplane over the Mardi Gras parades out over the Gulf to oblivion. Both extremes lead to destruction.

Those characters in between these extremes work out their destinies with more or less success. Dr. Muller goes off to a Health Services Convention, and Dr. Hunt goes back to India. Dr. Gomez leaves for Mexico, and the beginning of a new revolution. The father figures continue in their best developments. Fr. Victor, seeing the violent death of his old friend Joe Piavi, turns back to the order of the Church, deciding to compromise by offering an alternative to his original communal plan.

Finally, Jason, too, compromises; Susanna comes to his apartment late on Mardi Gras evening and tells him of her love. This human response is enough for him now; he decides to marry her, take up his father's practice from Dr. Gomez, and finish his treatise on *Kala-azar*. This is all a compromise, but a sensible, human compromise which in a sense allows Jason the best of all possible worlds, given the essential violence and chaos of the modern world.

This resolution also smacks just slightly of the conventional and commercial "happy ending" which mars some Basso novels, just as Susanna unfortunately seems too much the nice girl of the 1930s movies. Yet the novel's careful working out of this solution makes it much more acceptable than a short summary might indicate. The complexities of the human condition are not oversimplified, and Jason does not discover any ultimate answer to the great questions which modern life asks. Instead he finds a believable, workable, human compromise. The novel's rich dramatization of this essentially mature development, a maturation process often at the heart of Basso's books, combined with the greater intellectual complexity of the novel's ideas and themes, make this one of the author's finest novels, one which merited the Southern Authors Award.

II Wine of the Country

Basso's next novel, *Wine of the Country* (1941), is in many ways very similar to *Days Before Lent*. Again the protagonist fits the pattern of the Basso hero: Tait Ravenwill, possessing a

Romantic Southern name reminiscent of Dekker Blackheath's, is a Southerner, from the coastal country of South Carolina, a sensitive intellectual, in this case a young anthropologist, and a man about to choose his place in the world at the age of thirty. Again this choice involves vocation, marriage, and geographical setting. Even more than in the previous novel the choice is complicated by the dark cultural mood on the eve of World War II. In one sense, *Wine of the Country* is a stronger book than *Days Before Lent* because of its clear intellectual statement; in another sense it is weaker because its narrative is not only less dramatic, but also less integral to its themes. As often happens in his books, Basso is unable to find a structure which will adequately express his ideas, and *Wine of the Country* finally presents many interesting pieces, but not a coherent whole.

The author's ideas in this case are generally similar to those in his earlier novels. Man must find meaningful work, meaningful human relationships, and a meaningful balance with his environment. Various aspects of these ideas are presented by the father-figure characters in *Days Before Lent,* occasionally with an anthropological bias. In *Wine of the Country* they receive a definite anthropological treatment, as Basso's central character works in this field. The only important father figure here is Professor Prescott, author of *Science and Society,* the most important anthropological work of the day. When the novel opens, the older scholar is working on a new book, *Faith and Society,* which he intends as a text for the times. His thesis is that scientific anthropology can describe the decay of a culture, whether the primitive culture which Tait observed in his South Seas research, or the present disintegration of Europe, but anthropology as a humanistic study, implied in its very name, must have faith in man, both individual and social. This humanistic faith in man, almost a liberal dogma, can adequately compensate for the loss of religious faith which has afflicted modern man. There are several corollaries to this theory. Human relationships, particularly sexual and familial relationships, are of more importance than other social relationships. The primitive, even atavistic, side of man must be recognized and given its due. And, therefore, man's relationship to the physical environment in which he lives will become more important.

At first glance, the narrative line of the novel seems well designed to illustrate these ideas. Basso, of course, has plenty of opportunity for his two anthropologists to state them directly in reading, writing, and conversation, including debate, because the older man must convince the younger of his ideas about human faith. The other activities of the young anthropologist also provide dramatic exemplification. Dr. Prescott has three daughters and a niece he has adopted as a daughter after his brother's death. The niece, Ellen, is a strange, near-hysterical girl of twenty-five who has been bitterly disappointed in her first love and has reacted with bitterness and cynicism toward life in general. Her fiancé had a baby by an Irish servant girl, and Ellen repays him by having a shabby affair with a cheap Irish politico from Boston. Catherine, the oldest daughter, at twenty-four, seems sensible enough, but she too has been moody since the death of her mother, and she rejects all men less intelligent than her father. Elizabeth, twenty-three, is the most beautiful of the girls; she shocks the family by choosing a career as a nightclub singer. The youngest daughter, Jean, twenty-one and just graduated from Smith, opts for financial security by marrying a rich Boston banker, the forty-five-year-old guardian of one of her classmates. Certainly, the girls' developing histories provide Professor Prescott with considerable exemplification for his theories about the disintegration of cultural order.

Tait Ravenwill's family background also promises apt examples of social decay. The Ravenwills are a typically Faulknerian family, once rich, now genteelly middle class, trying to hold together the old house and plantation in Tidewater South Carolina. However, they are far from the *Gone With the Wind* vision of the Southern aristocracy; instead their desolate stretch of the Carolina coast seems a tropical jungle more like Cuba or Africa than Charlestown or Savannah. Malarial swamps are full of wild game; the voodoo doctors still practice among the Gullah-speaking blacks; and the whites scratch out a living growing cane, rice, and tropical flowers. Into this atmosphere of decay Tait is born; he works his way out through the academic life, but he is always drawn back as if by the aroma of some wine distilled from the fecund earth itself. His brother Ned, a year or two younger, has already given himself over to the pull of raw nature, chucking his promising career as a painter in New York to return home, raise flowers for the Northern markets, and spend his time hunting and fishing. Ned is somewhat akin to Ellen Prescott, in that he has been broken by the traumatic experience of his first love, who was killed in a hunting accident. He is married to a gentle, understanding woman, Marion, but he wildly seeks death in his hunt for Old Red, the giant deer he was stalking when his young fiancée was killed.

It is the linking of these two disintegrating families which creates the major problems of the novel. Tait, back from a two-year research trip in the South Seas, stops to see Dr. Prescott for advice about writing his book. Prescott, of course, brings him home for dinner, and he has a choice of romantic attractions among the Prescott girls. He knows Catherine is the more admirable, but something in his emotional makeup responds to the dark, tragic force in Ellen, a force which seems almost a doomed sexuality. Catherine hesitates in her feelings for Tait, afraid that the young Southerner cannot come up to the standards of her father. Ellen, in contrast, gives herself passionately to him at the first opportunity. Catherine appeals to and represents the intellectual and moral side of Tait; Ellen, the physical and emotional. Tait is already tending toward the more primitive virtues, as he has become convinced that the intellectual and especially the academic life are essentially empty and meaningless. Thus he marries Ellen after a short courtship, endures Chadhurst College until the end of the academic year, and then packs off to Three Crow Corners, South Carolina, in order to finish his book.

The shift in locale gives the novel a considerable life, for the Massachusetts scenes were weakly, imperfectly rendered. The minor characters are almost exclusively stereotypes, from the incredibly named Boston wardheeler, Kenneth O'Kelley, to the good Dr. Prescott, a stock figure of the absentminded professor. Of course, a household packed by four Basso heroines, all young, beautiful, and proper is almost more than the reader can stand. The only other important characters are the girls' various suitors, all one-dimensional drawings. They include Mr. Logan, Jean's banker; Colin, Elizabeth's New England aesthete; as well as Catherine's paired suitors, Tom Wickliffe, an amiable ex-football player, and Knox Peters, a sour history instructor. As with the New York scenes in *Courthouse Square*, Basso is also unable to render New England.

However, South Carolina is well handled. The wild country, the decadent society, the colorful individuals all seem interesting and credible. Ned Ravenwill is one of Basso's best characterizations. The deaf and somewhat senile Edward Ravenwill, Tait and

Ned's father, is a fully believable character, as are the other members of the family: Marion, Ned's wife; Uncle Jack; and the acerbic Dr. Sharpe. The other important family of the region, the Blakes, include Cynthia, Tait's old flame, a Southern belle of simmering sexuality; and Harry Blake, her older brother, who falls in love with Ellen. The black characters play minor roles, but they are realistically presented, particularly Cash, Ned's hunting companion.

Once in South Carolina, Ellen begins to disintegrate. It seems as if her precarious emotional balance is upset by an environment so completely oriented toward her weaker side, as everything in Three Corners is primitive, physical, and emotional. Ellen is oppressed by the heat, frightened of the insect and animal life, made nervous by the incomprehensible blacks, puzzled by her in-laws and their friends, and frustrated with her new husband. She resents Tait's long hours with his book, and the time he spends hunting and fishing with Ned. She easily becomes jealous of Tait's old love, Cynthia Blake, who obviously still has her eye on him, married or not. Three events—a dove hunt, a cockfight, and Ned's releasing of a raccoon in the house—mark her growing hysteria in this strange, almost primitive, world. When Tait announces that he has decided to give up his career in anthropology and join Ned in running the plantation, Ellen breaks at the prospect of permanence in Three Corners.

Tait then asks Catherine to visit and perhaps take Ellen back to New England for a few months while he finishes his book. Catherine, of course, agrees, and when she arrives in South Carolina all the Ravenwills are charmed with her. Tait more and more realizes that Catherine would have made him a better wife, as an anthropologist or as a farmer. Her intellectual nature balances nicely with the mindlessness of the Ravenwill's country. Catherine, for her part, still feels strongly attracted to Tait, though she, of course, would do nothing to hurt Ellen. During Catherine's visit Ellen becomes more and more despondent over her situation, and she even begins to be jealous of her cousin. One evening Tait is showing Catherine around the garden, while Ellen is resting from an argument with him she had that afternoon. The "wine of the country," redolent of moonlight and magnolias, goes to Catherine's head, and she yields to Tait's romantic advances. Ellen comes on them kissing in the garden, becomes completely hysterical, and runs off into the swamp where she eventually becomes hopelessly lost and dies of exposure during a tropical storm.

A short coda chapter narrates the events of the year after Ellen's death. A few months after that unhappy event, Ned was also killed, locked in a death struggle with Old Red. Of course, it is appropriate that both characters die such wild deaths in the midst of the wilderness. Tait, in revulsion from the primitive impulses which have killed his wife and brother, goes back to his anthropological studies, completes his book, and begins another on the Gullah blacks of the Three Crow Corners region. The Prescotts continue in their set courses, notably Catherine in her patient wait for the time she can go to Ravenwill. Thus the conclusion posits in typical Basso terms the possibility of order, both intellectual and emotional, restored in the future.

It is an irony outside the book that America's entrance into World War II must have followed hard on Tait's final letter to Catherine, as the novel was published in the autumn of 1941. Speculation about the effect of war's disorder on the precarious balances struck by the conclusion of the novel are literarily pointless, though interesting. More to the point are other limiting factors existing within the novel itself. The most obvious is the substitution of Catherine for Ellen. Would the change of cousins really make that much difference in Tait's situation? Given the typically vague delineation of Catherine, the thoughtful reader must really pause and wonder. Although Tait seems to think Catherine a very strong person, no evidence of this strength is really advanced. Catherine, like the Basso heroines of other books, seems a reasonably nice girl, and she did get along with the Ravenwills during her visit. Yet would she really fare any better than Ellen in the isolation and stagnation of Three Crow Corners? The question is moot, but it certainly weakens the effectiveness of Basso's conclusion. Once again, the author tries to resolve complicated and difficult problems with a Hollywood ending of "then they lived happily ever after."

In a sense this typical problem of Basso's conclusion is only the tip of the iceberg in terms of this novel's difficulties, ones which ultimately sink it as successful fiction. In a sense the whole romantic narrative of the love for two women seems clichéd as well as divorced from the themes of the novel. Ellen does represent the disorder of the modern world in some way, but it is not clear how. Basso finally can make her wild disorder understandable only in terms of a basic emotional or mental instability, but this disorder is only tenuously connected with the more universal problems of the culture. The early death of her parents, the shameless treatment by her fiancé, the difficulty of isolation in an alien backwater, and her own lack of balance are not really good correlatives for the destructive forces which were at the same time destroying civilization in Europe and Asia.

Likewise, Tait's pivotal role in the novel, his choice between the two women and the consequences of his choice, present added problems. How is Tait's attraction to Ellen indicative of a cultural breakdown? Making a young woman who has had one unfortunate affair representative of the disintegration of morality, faith, and civilization is quite simply a mistake. On the other hand, resolving this difficulty by marrying a girl who has not had an affair seems just as weak in moral terms. Put simply, Basso's themes, raised in the elevated dialogue between the anthropologists, and his story of Tait's two loves, are not integrated. The result is the blurring of a novel of ideas with the popular romance, which sometimes was Basso's greatest weakness.

Not that the novel is a complete failure. The flow of ideas proves interesting, even if somewhat lost in the convolutions of the romantic plot. Basso's heart and head are obviously in the right place in terms of the difficulties of the day. These ideas are not as diverse as those which inform *Days Before Lent*, but they are more carefully organized and lucidly stated. The other side of the anthropologists' work, the illustration of their basic theories of culture in examples from fieldwork, is also quite interesting. The reminiscences of the two men about expeditions in the Pacific, in Central America, and among the American Indians add a good deal of color to the book. Basso was becoming the excellent travel writer who would later publish regularly in this area.

Also, the depiction of the decaying, small-town South is quite well done. The description of coastal South Carolina is fine writing about place, especially in the scenes of hunting and fishing. In fact, Ned's hunt for Old Red is one of the best pieces of narrative in all of Basso's works, almost as good as the story of the *Kala-azar* epidemic in his previous novel. The hunting sequences prefigure his fine hunting stories which would be written later for the *New Yorker*, and these hunting descriptions all deserve comparison with Faulkner's similar work in *Go Down, Moses* (1942). The characters in Three Crow Corners are for the most part well handled and very believable. The difficulty with this whole section of the novel is evident in the title of Book II, "The Vintage." Book I, the New England scene, was entitled "The Vine." The connection is tenuous and the plotting fails to make the connection, as demonstrated above. Unfortunately, the South exists in this novel only as a place for the Northern vintage to sour; it does not exist for itself and is not probed for its own meaning, as in the best of Basso's novels.

In summary, *Wine of the Country* can be viewed as a typical Basso novel, one which connects especially with *Days Before Lent*, which precedes it, and *Sun In Capricorn*, which follows it. The novel presents interesting ideas about the contemporary cultural situation through the agency of the protagonist's intellectual interests as an anthropologist. The narrative of his personal development, however, does not stress his connection with vocational father figures, as in *Days Before Lent*, but with a number of romantic interests. Thus plot leads Basso into his weakest area, and away from his strongest. More importantly, it provides little integration of idea and action, creating an unbalanced and unsatisfying fictional work. Basso's ideas and some parts of his narrative, notably the hunting scenes in South Carolina, are well handled, but overall the novel fails to become a coherent whole. Finally, the book must be judged one of the author's less successful efforts.

III Sun In Capricorn

Basso's next novel, *Sun In Capricorn* (1942), has received more scholarly attention than any of his other books; this attention undoubtedly results from the novel's subject matter—the life and times of Huey Long—than from its art. The novel is not one of Basso's best. Although the subject proves interesting, Basso was perhaps too close to develop it properly; the author takes a very narrow view of Long in his fictional recreation as Gilgo Slade. A personality as complex as Long's needs a broad canvas for a full portrait—witness T. Harry Williams's recent biography of Long, or Robert Penn Warren's fictional biography of Willie Stark in *All The King's Men*.[2] Basso's novel is one of his shortest, and, as usual, it centers on the Basso protagonist, in this case, a young Louisiana lawyer named Hazzard. As in other novels, Basso does not discover a fictional structure which links his disparate strands of plot, and *Sun In Capricorn* fragments as a political novel and a romantic thriller.

Hazzard, though a believable character, lacks the complexity of Jason Kent or Tait Ravenwill. He is more of a throwback to Tony Clezac and Dekker Blackheath of the early novels, or to David Barondess of *Courthouse Square*. Even in comparison to these characters, Hazzard lacks a certain vitality, perhaps because his creator seems to model him on the earlier versions. The fictional creations of other writers also enter his makeup. The novel is presented from a first-person perspective, and early in his description of himself Hazzard tells the reader:

It may be that in those impressionable years of my youth my father over-taught the lesson of tolerance, or it may be some fault of my own, but it has always been possible for me to like certain people without admiring them. This has brought me some curious friendships, and made me the victim of I don't know how many bores, since a mere lack of standards and values does not make a man likable or entertaining, but I have discovered that the continents of the moral world are very thinly peopled and that if you insist upon communing only with the inhabitants of that country you are apt to find yourself dwelling in a loneliness no less desolate because it is superior. (18-19)

The passage seems very close to Nick Carraway's description of his own sensibilities at the opening of *The Great Gatsby,* and in overall personality Hazzard seems somewhat based on Nick.

Unlike the earlier versions of the Basso protagonists, Hazzard exists primarily in a symbolic pairing with another character; for if Hazzard is Nick, Gilgo Slade is his Gatsby. The problem is that he becomes no "great Gilgo." Rather Slade is a completely reprehensible demagogue, a figure of almost consummate evil. By making Gilgo into a villainous antagonist for his central character, Basso loses much of the interest inherent in Huey Long's story, and turns what should be a realistic novel into melodrama. Hazzard becomes a simpler version of Jason and Tait of the previous novels, a good man trying to find the right direction for his life within the dangers and difficulties of the modern world. Unlike Jason he has only two paternal surrogates to choose between; Gilgo, representing a bad choice, and his Uncle Thomas, representing a good one. He makes his rather easy choice, and opposes the evil of his time, a sort of home-grown Fascism, but the drama of his decision is much less effective than the complex maturations of Basso's earlier protagonists.

Hazzard is cut from the same cloth, however. His father is a half-French, half-Italian schoolteacher from New Orleans who came to the northern Louisiana parish of Montrose to run the venerable Montrose Academy, founded before the Civil War by Edward Hazzard. He married a local belle, the last of the Hazzards, and had one son, who is given his mother's family name. (Curiously, the reader never learns the narrator's family name.) The mother died when young Hazzard was seven, and the father moved back to New Orleans. Here Hazzard led a life much like Dekker Blackheath's or Jason Kent's until he was twelve and his father died. Hazzard then went to live with his mother's sister, Aunt Caroline, and her lawyer husband, Uncle Thomas, in their home, the restored Hazzard Hall. They have one son, Quentin, who is just Hazzard's age, and the boys spend their time hunting and fishing with a young black boy, Trowel. Hazzard and Quentin also attend Montrose Academy, and after graduation they go off respectively to Yale and Princeton, from which they come back educated as, respectively, a lawyer and a banker.

The only other event of importance in Hazzard's life occurred when he was fifteen; he fell in love with his beautiful young cousin, Augusta Lowndes, and he stays in love with her until he is thirty. In the meantime, he has a serious relationship with a Smith College girl, Sandra Miller, but he is fascinated by the *belle dame sans merci*, Augusta. He has actually come back to the sleepy town of Montrose only to be near her, and he stays on even after she marries a richer man, Corliss Blake. His inability to grow beyond his adolescent fascination for Augusta symbolizes his overall immaturity. He makes just enough money practicing small-town law to buy a farm outside of town, where Trowel and his wife, Cordelia, are hired as handyman and housekeeper. Hazzard then settles into a lassitudinous routine of hunting and fishing, playing the guitar, and raising mules. At the point where the novel opens he has decided to give up the law entirely and live on the income from his livestock. Thus he repudiates the intellectual heritage of his father (Montrose Academy has closed since he has returned from college), the

legal heritage of his uncle, and the aristocratic heritage of his
aunt (the last of the Hazzards) and his cousin.

In one sense he has allied himself with Gilgo Slade. The
politician is from a farm background in a nearby parish, and he is
given to emphasizing his "downhome" origins. He sponsors
fishfries, country music jamborees, and livestock exhibitions as
part of his campaign tactics. Yet, in a real sense, Gilgo goes
beyond all of this. He is self-educated, a lawyer by special
examination, and the new Snopesian aristocrat of false merit.
Therefore, Hazzard in his development is allying himself with
what seems good in Gilgo, the simple, rural world of the past.
But, like so many of his fellow citizens, he is allowing Gilgo to
swindle him in the modern world of power politics. Hazzard is
aware of Gilgo's two sides to some extent; he first respects him as
a populist, then loses that respect when he sees what a
demagogue Gilgo really is. However, he chooses to ignore rather
than to oppose him.

In these positions Hazzard is close to his creator, Hamilton
Basso. In several articles written for the *New Republic* during the
1930s, Basso confessed that he at first admired Long as a
welcome antidote to the so-called "New Orleans Gang" who had
run the state before him.[3] The liberal journalist soon became
disenchanted with "The Kingfish" when he started to employ
unscrupulous means to achieve his ends. In Basso's view Long
then abandoned his great democratic potential; ". . . he
deliberately turned away, in willful ambitious pride, and sought
to build a lower kingdom of his own."[4] It is easy to understand
Basso's feelings, and, indeed, his judgment was the general one
on Long in the 1930s. But modern historical scholarship, in
particular T. Harry William's definitive biography, has presented
a more positive image of Long, which while admitting his
personal ambition, totalitarian tactics, and bad taste, still puts
more stress on his populist origins, his real achievements in
Louisiana, and his forward-looking programs.

Basso creates a greater problem by recreating Huey Long as
Gilgo Slade. His portrait is without shading, as the positive side
of Slade is hardly mentioned. He is viewed entirely through the
perspective of old-guard politicians and old-line aristocrats, a
very narrow view. He finally becomes only a menacing,
monstrous antagonist to the novel's heroic antagonist, thus
reducing the story to melodrama. At least three other novels

were based on the career of Huey Long; it proves instructive to compare them. The novels which oversimplify Long are all second rate as literature.

Adria Locke Langly's *A Lion Is in the Streets* idealizes Long; John Dos Passos's *Number One* and Basso's *Sun In Capricorn* both denigrate him. Only Robert Penn Warren's *All the King's Men* (1946) treats Long as an ambivalent figure, and it is one of the finest novels produced in the Southern Renaissance.[5] Warren's Willie Stark is a great man, but one who loses his greatness in a tragic fall. Warren's Jack Burden is a man who labors to understand history and thus to plan the future. Basso protested Warren's treatment of Long, though admitting the consummate artistry of the book; his argument was that Huey Long was a figure dangerous to democracy, and thus to say anything good about him was socially irresponsible. Strangely, his position in 1946 begins to sound quite a bit like the proletarian position he rejected in the 1930s; either follow the party line or don't write!

Still, for all the oversimplification, Gilgo Slade is a colorful, dramatic character, and the parts of the novel which deal with him are much more interesting than those centered on Hazzard. When the novel opens Gilgo has just declared that he is going to run for the Senate, and the old guard has nominated Hazzard's Uncle Thomas, once a popular and successful U.S. Representative, to oppose him. His uncle is too busy with politics to keep up with all his legal business, so Hazzard postpones his retirement from the law firm and travels to New Orleans to do some of their business. There he runs into Fritz Cowan, a man of his own age from Montrose, a one-time suitor of Augusta, who has hitched his wagon to Gilgo's ascending political star. Cowan buys Hazzard lunch and offers him the congressional seat which his uncle held if the young lawyer will come over to the Slade camp. Hazzard, of course, refuses, but he does come along to one of Gilgo's political meetings.

The chapter which describes this outlandish event is a *tour de force* reminiscent of Gatsby's great parties. Held in Gilgo's suite of apartments, it is more of a social event than a political meeting. Gilgo appears in monogrammed green silk pajamas and spends most of his time interviewing drum majorettes and fireeaters for his circuslike campaign rallies. The whole affair has a mad, dreamlike unreality which fascinates Hazzard so that he cannot pull away in spite of himself. When Fritz leaves him to his own devices, Hazzard falls in with a Mr. Dent, a depressed dentist who represents the kind of poor soul who attaches himself to a "great man" like Gilgo. Gilgo declared a moratorium on mortgages which saved his home and office, and Dent will be eternally subservient to Gilgo's politics.

The other denizens of the governor's apartments are a crew as strange as those at Gatsby's bizarre evenings. In fact, the guest list is similar to the one that Nick writes on an old timetable in *The Great Gatsby.*

The crowd about the bar grew thicker. I was introduced to Mr. McAllister Jones of Athens, Georgia, and the brothers T. R. and R. T. Beam of Union Springs, Alabama, and Mr. Charlie Arnstein, the famous slotmachine distributor of New York and Chicago. "It's a pleasure, gentlemen," he kept saying. "It's a perfect pleasure," and it was hard to believe what Mr. Thorndike Peele, the racing man who was president of Sunset Oil Operatives, Inc., said about him when he left to join the crapgame—that, in Chicago, he was more dreaded than Al Capone. I also met Donald Dorne, the New Orleans poet who wrote a gossip column for Gilgo's weekly newspaper, and with him there was Leonard K. Young, the advertising agent, as well as the Mexican painter, Francisco Pedro Gonzales, who asked Fritz Cowan if he had spoken to Gilgo about the matter of the murals for the new State Capitol building. (75)

Hazzard drinks and talks with this group until Gilgo himself arrives and then all are silent while "The Boss" dictates a slanderous editorial to one of his newspapers, attacking Uncle Thomas as a crook and a carpetbagger. At this point Hazzard leaves.

That night he meets Erin, the novel's love interest and the typically "right girl" for the Basso protagonist. Erin is a slightly more interesting version of this now familiar type: she is Irish, independent of mind, and divorced. Her love proves a good deal more corporeal than that of other Basso heroines, and she is almost believable as a character. A contemporary lady reviewer, Gwen Bristow, writing in the *Saturday Review,* wittily rendered the difficulty Basso created in this aspect of the novel.

It's not all as good as this. When the young man meets the girl and falls in love with her, Mr. Basso seems to get embarrassed about the whole business. Like a flustered speechmaker,, he says the same things over and over till the audience gets embarrassed too. At their first meeting, the narrator asks the girl a question and then says, "She nodded her chin." A little later, he observes, "She made a small noncommital sound." A few pages further on, he describes her smile by saying "She crinkled her nose at me." Apparently he liked these sentences. For he keeps repeating their phrases. The girl's nodding chin, her crinkling nose, and her small sounds get so monotonous that the reader is happy to get back to Slade and his evil but interesting behavior.[6]

Basso must be excused somewhat because he is compelled by the necessities of his plot to describe that most elusive of emotions — "love at first sight." Erin's sexuality makes it more believable than in his other books, but the reader still finds it hard to believe that the couple are in love the first night they meet, in bed the second, and on the run with each other the third.

The reason they have to run is that Fritz Cowan had Hazzard followed, and he attempts to blackmail him with evidence of his night with Erin, a violation of the rarely enforced moral codes, which still can be used to harass political enemies. Hazzard takes Erin back to Montrose and hides her in the abandoned academy while he makes plans to send her north, after making some explanation to his family and planning a legal campaign against Gilgo's harassment. The symbolism of the abandoned house come back to life recalls *Courthouse Square*. Hazzard is back in his father's tradition; his legal plans put him in his uncle's tradition also, and soon he will be thinking like his cousin. Quentin feels that the family honor has been impugned; he first threatens Hazzard, and then, learning that the newspaper story is a lie, he swears vengeance on Cowan and Gilgo. Hazzard cautions him and sets out with Erin to put her on a northbound train.

Unfortunately, he runs into the heavy traffic for Gilgo's political rally in a neighboring town, is forced to enter the fairgrounds where the rally is to be held, is there recognized, arrested, and forced to wait while Gilgo does his act. The carnival-like political rally provides another dramatic *tour de force*, which in fact had been planned at the earlier meeting. As Gilgo goes through his entertaining antics, Hazzard contemplates grabbing the pistol of the state policeman who is guarding him and assassinating the would-be senator. Just as he has himself talked into this hysterical act, another shot rings out, and Gilgo falls, a bullet in his head. Quentin has gunned the demagogue down in a mistaken defense of his family's honor. He is, in turn, immediately cut down by Gilgo's bodyguards, and the catastrophe is complete. In a short coda, Mr. Dent commits suicide in despair; Gilgo is buried; Quentin is judged temporarily insane; Uncle Thomas withdraws from the senate race; and Hazzard is released from all charges. Thus he is left free to marry Erin and assume his rightful place as the intellectual, legal, and social leader of Montrose. Now that he knows that he cannot run away from responsibility, he is ready to assume it, and with it his full maturity.

The general pattern of the book is close to that of other Basso novels, both the group of early works and the two books of the prewar period. A sensitive young Southerner matures, learns his place in the world, and settles down to a productive life. In this case the dramatic complications of Gilgo Slade's brand of homegrown Fascism makes an interesting background for the central character's development. Yet the novel finally wastes this material because of the author's inability to render it in terms of thematic complexity. As pointed out above, the novel bears more than a little resemblance to *The Great Gatsby*. Like Fitzgerald's novel, it is a compact, dramatic narrative, well told by a sensitive protagonist, which involves a colorful, corrupt, and finally violent background. The deficiency of Basso's novel is that the symbolic character does not attain the complexity and human mystery of Jay Gatsby; instead he is a purely villainous antagonist for a protagonist a good deal less well drawn than Nick Carraway, or for that matter Basso's earlier heroes such as Jason Kent or David Barondess. Robert Penn Warren's *All the King's Men*, also influenced by Fitzgerald's greatest novel, does employ the history of Huey Long very successfully; Basso's book, because of the writer's problems of thematic conception and fictional craft, does not. At the same time it must be recognized that *Sun In Capricorn* falters only in comparison with this truly great novel; in its own terms it is a small success, as contemporary reviewers found it. It is interesting, well written, and often exciting, but it is not the great book Basso might have written about Huey Long.

CHAPTER 5

The Non-Southern Novels

THIS chapter alters the chronological sequence of Basso's novels; although it first considers Basso's next novel, *The Greenroom* (1949), it then skips past the Pompey's Head novels to his last book, *A Touch of the Dragon* (1964). The logic behind the conjunction of these novels, written fifteen years apart, is twofold: first, since the novels are separate chronologically from any others by at least five years, it seems feasible to link them; second, and more importantly, the two books present parallels of theme and character which make it sensible to pair them. Both books, though employing the now familiar Basso protagonists, center on women as antagonists. Also, both are set outside the South, and neither depicts an important Southern character. Even the final evaluation of both novels proves intriguing, though contrastive; *The Greenroom* is, perhaps, Basso's best single novel; *A Touch of the Dragon* is, perhaps, his worst. The analysis which follows will establish the reasons for these judgments in a close reading of the two books.

I The Greenroom

The success of *The Greenroom* can be explained at least partially in terms of its position within the Basso canon. After *Sun In Capricorn* was published in 1942, Basso did not publish a novel for seven years. Undoubtedly, the tensions of the war years and Basso's increasing responsibilities as family man and professional journalist at least partially account for this long hiatus. During this period the author wrote and published a great deal, mostly nonfiction, but also some short stories, a genre he had more or less ignored earlier. *The Greenroom* is loosely based on prewar experiences in the South of France; there is some indication that Basso began the book soon after the war, but that

91

the work went slowly. Again, his responsibilities probably cut into his writing time, and, more importantly, the novel is more carefully crafted and written than the earlier ones. His final three novels also had fairly lengthy gestation periods. In any case, *The Greenroom* was written when Basso was at the height of his powers; well settled, with few pressures—personal, professional, or ideological—to rush the work, he was able to produce a fine book.

The thematic relationship of the novel to the Basso canon also partially accounts for its success. *The Greenroom* is Basso's only novel to be set in another country, the only novel aside from *A Touch of the Dragon* to be set completely outside of the South. Even the protagonist, though generally within the outlines of the Basso hero seen in the earlier books, is not a Southerner; nor are any of the main characters. More importantly, the second character, the antagonist, is a woman, a complex, fully developed, lady novelist. The relationship which develops between these characters creates thematic emphases not found in the other books and opens up dramatic possibilities for the author which he misses elsewhere. In particular, he stresses American, rather than Southern themes, as he contrasts an older, richer culture with America's. Of course, this study has stressed Basso's importance as a writer of the Southern Renaissance, and the accumulated power of the nine Southern novels makes *The Greenroom* seem something of a side trip for his talent. Yet *The Greenroom* proves the most interesting, the most carefully crafted, and the most completely successful of his novels.

Some of Basso's success in *The Greenroom* must be accorded to his literary models. Just as the form and feeling of *The Great Gatsby* informed *Sun In Capricorn*, so another great American novel influenced *The Greenroom;* in this case the book is Henry James's *The American.* Basso had always appreciated the work of America's greatest Realist, and Jamesian suggestions are found in several of his books, most notably the character of Pierson James of *In Their Own Image.* The author's decision to write about a European setting undoubtedly brought him back to the works of the "Master," and James has no more popular or accessible novel than *The American* (1877). It tells the story of Christopher Newman, self-made American millionaire, who retires at thirty-five to Europe and the "good life." In France he discovers that the truly successful life is more difficult to attain than he had previously imagined. In particular, he is thwarted in his love for the beautiful and pure heroine, Claire, by her haughty, unscrupulous family, the Bellegardes.

In broad outline Basso's story resembles James's. Rufus Jackson (a name as definitely American as Christopher Newman), born and educated in Arizona, once a playwright, now a New York assistant editor, vacations in France where he learns the full complexities of the mature life through his relationship with two women, Mrs. Leslie Porter, an aged lady novelist, and her niece by marriage, Nora Marsh. Like Newman, Jackson tries to marry this beautiful, sophisticated foreign girl, but he is frustrated by her prideful family, in this case Mrs. Porter and her nephew, Charles Marsh. Other less central characters are right out of James also, particularly the worldly Princess de Cloville and her dying lover, the Marquis. The theme is more Jamesian than plot or character, however; American naiveté is tried and found wanting, but the American hero, only thirty-seven at the novel's close, has a chance to redeem himself in the world of art.

Jackson, though his background is made Western, hence even more American, is the typical Basso protagonist. Sensitive, intelligent, and liberal, he is a spokesman for the author's ideas and to some extent an autobiographical portrait. The same age as Basso when he was in France, Jackson is similarly a writer who has met with moderate success and drifted into another field. Unlike Basso he is a widower, which provides the novel's romance interest. As usual, this is the least successful part of the book, though the reader at least escapes a perfunctory "they lived happily ever after" conclusion. More important and better handled than Jackson's romance with Nora is his education at the chateau of Mrs. Porter, an experience which has greater biographical and fictional reality.

The formidable Mrs. Porter, though bearing the name of a famous Southern writer, is more likely based on the Jamesian protégé Edith Wharton, who died at her French chateau in 1937. There are, of course, many differences between the model and the character, but there are too many resemblances to go unnoticed. Both were young ladies of a somewhat socially undistinguished background who nevertheless captivated New York and Newport before the turn of the century. Both were married, somewhat unhappily, to older, wealthy men, who indulged them in their writing, and did not give them children.

Both turned out a number of distinguished fictional works depicting the old-fashioned society of New York. Mrs. Porter achieved more recognition winning the Nobel Prize, yet both were critically successful and widely praised. Both were somewhat cold, reserved, self-centered figures who led some-what reclusive later lives in French *châteaux*. Undoubtedly Basso emphasized this side of his character in order to make her a symbol of another Jamesian theme—the isolation of the artist and the dangers of artistic success.

The portrait of Mrs. Leslie Porter is one of the most complex Basso attempted, as well as one of the most successfully accomplished. His earlier writing had to some extent prepared the reader for this character by his greater success with the depiction of older women, particularly the various aunts of his protagonists. Of course, Mrs. Porter is much different from these well-meaning Southern ladies, but they are in a sense her fictional forebears. So are the father-figure characters of the earlier novels; the portraits of artistically, or at least intellec-tually, successful men such as John Pine of *In Their Own Image* or Dr. Hunt of *Days Before Lent* are somewhat similar to Mrs. Porter. For this lady is a very formidable person in both an artistic and an intellectual sense. She is possessed of a fine mind, an indomitable will, and a great store of social charm. What she lacks is precisely those qualities which make the Southern aunts so appealing—warmth, emotion, understanding. In order to make herself an artistic success, Mrs. Porter has stifled these qualities in herself; she writes to compensate for an unhappy life, and though she creates masterful fictions she cannot make her personal life creative in any sense. Her husband did not love her; her lover would not stay with her; her nephew, adopted by the childless widow, is nearly destroyed by her. This, then, is the paradox of the artistic career of Mrs. Leslie Porter.

It is also the source of the novel's title, *The Greenroom*. The term is taken from the opening line of Mrs. Porter's most famous work, *The Chronicles of Catherine*. "She began each day with a rehearsal, closeted in the greenroom of her soul." In case the reader misses the message Basso attaches the dictionary definition of greenroom: "A room in a theatre for actors and actresses when not required on the stage."[1] Mrs. Porter's description of the autobiographical Catherine extends easily to the authoress herself; though in her seventies, in the greenroom of life, as it were, she still begins each day with a rehearsal of the play where she is heroine and in which she forces those around her to act. This knowledge is the key to her character, as Jackson realizes toward the end of the novel, and says of this epigraph:

He recalled the opening line of what was generally considered her finest book, *The Chronicles of Catherine.* It was perhaps the most famous line she had ever written: "She began each day with a rehearsal, closeted in the greenroom of her soul." It was almost too apt, he thought; too easy and convenient a key. But because of it, and also because he felt he had at last come to the point where he could see her for what she was—an aging woman who would not yield to her age, given to endless histrionics, insanely jealous of Nora for being all the things she herself no longer was—he was able to confront her calmly. (235)

Basso cannot be accused of slighting her great literary success; Jackson as well as all the other characters admit that she is a great novelist. But Mrs. Porter herself insists, "Along with being a writer I am a woman—that I am a woman *before* I am a writer" (240). As a writer she is a success, as a woman a failure.

Unfortunately, Basso somewhat fails in his purposes because the woman she is most completely contrasted with, Nora Marsh, proves, as usual with the Basso heroine, a failure. Basso was to some extent improving the breed; Nora, like Erin of *Sun In Capricorn,* has at least a corporeal reality. She is separated from her husband, and she is willing to respond sexually to Jackson. But the description of their lovemaking sets the tone of the relationship. "The avalanche had thundered, the earth had pitched and rolled, the night had blazed with a hundred suns" (212). The reader can hardly accept this clichéd heroine as a viable alternative to the well-drawn Mrs. Porter.

Fortunately, Basso saves the novel by presenting another feminine foil to Mrs. Porter, the Princess de Cloville. The princess is nearly Mrs. Porter's age; she is physically repulsive, and her life seems much less successful. She has been married a number of times, taken even more lovers, gambled away her family fortune, and created no lasting work of any sort. Yet for all of this the princess is a more human and likable figure than Mrs. Porter. At the opening of the novel she has come to be with her dying lover, the aged Marquis de Vernay. Their union at his death is in direct contrast to Mrs. Porter's loneliness when her lover, Philip Lenox, announces that he is going off to live with his married daughter in Australia. The princess is a wonderful character, out of Henry James's pages, who has seen the evil of the world and even participated in it, taking her chances at roulette and life, yet keeping her essential humanity, something which Mrs. Porter has sold away for literary success.

Basso creates another contrastive character to indicate that Mrs. Porter's personal failure was not a necessary condition of artistic achievement. Oliver Winyard, a literary friend of Mrs. Porter's, is a little-known American expatriate novelist and essayist. Although he has enjoyed less success than his Nobel Prize-winning friend, Jackson judges him as a fine or perhaps an even finer writer. Yet Winyard is a sort of refined, male version of the princess. Worldly, irascible, and hard-drinking, he still is a part of the fallen world of ordinary humanity in a way Mrs. Porter is not. It is important that he alone recognizes the source of her nephew's weaknesses, especially his alcoholism, in Mrs. Porter's domineering attitude toward him.

Winyard also serves as foil for Jackson, the failed playwright, and the other characters of any importance fulfill similar functions. Spike Carruthers is another American expatriate, a broken-down journalist wandering Europe in a drunken stupor and gathering material for a picaresque novel about a Fuller Brush man (a cliché of the period). Carruthers provides some rather good comic relief, something Basso doesn't always handle well. In the international spectrum he plays a more serious role as the ubiquitous "ugly American" with no sense of history or responsibility. In contrast to him, Jean Prudhomme, a young French professional man staying at Jackson's hotel, constantly worries about the pressures of history and the onset of war. He is completely immobilized by his neurotic dread of the future, thus, together with Charles Marsh, demonstrating that Rufus Jackson, the archetypal good American, is not such a bad sort in the balances he strikes.

The novel's plot likewise establishes Jackson's strength, humanity, and resilience. The book opens in late March of 1938 at a small town in Provence, ten or twelve miles inland from Nice. Rufus Jackson has come to Provence for a well-deserved vacation from his labors as a New York editor, and he has come to Paul's Hotel, a refurbished country inn, to pay a call on Mrs. Leslie Porter, one of his firm's more important writers. Mrs.

Porter had been writing her memoirs for a number of years after a $10,000 advance, and the chief editor, Charles Shannon, is beginning to get worried about ever receiving them. Jackson's mission is to inquire after the memoirs as diplomatically as possible (for Mrs. Porter has a fearsome temper) and to enjoy himself for another week before returning to the rigors of New York.

In Chapter 1, Rufus is found waiting for the hired car which will take him to tea at Mrs. Porter's. After arriving at Paul's Hotel, Jackson dropped the lady a note, asking to see her, half hoping that she might refuse him. Now he is rather glum at the prospect of a difficult hour with this formidable personage. While waiting for the car, he carries on a desultory conversation with an old villager, a sort of cynical peasant who represents the European point of view. Over and over again he chides Jackson for his national immaturity.

"That is because of the American immaturity," the old man answered. "I have watched many Americans, all those who came to the village, and they all have the same quality of immaturity. They come here, and they see a house that is four hundred years old, and immediately they cry, 'Look! See the house! It is four hundred years old!' In all Americans there is this same immaturity. I find it, too, hard to understand." (5)

The knowledge of history has made the European mature in a way which the American cannot understand until he has lived through a similar experience. The development of the novel will provide such experiences for Rufus Jackson.

The tea party at Mrs. Porter's, a rather Jamesian social event, provides further exemplification of Jackson's general immaturity. When his car finally arrives, out stumbles Spike Carruthers, already drunk in the middle of the afternoon. What is worse, he immediately identifies with Jackson and insists they will be friends. When Jackson finally shakes him and arrives at Mrs. Porter's *château*, he is snubbed by the butler, patronized by Mrs. Porter, and ignored by the other guests, including the niece, Nora Marsh. When Mrs. Porter hears that he is from Arizona, she immediately typecasts him as a cowboy and introduces him as such to each person he meets. In a Jamesian sense Rufus Jackson still is the "cowboy," the confident young man who thinks he can finally force the world to yield him the happiness he has lost in the death of his wife and the failure of his playwriting.

The day after the tea party Jackson is awakened by a call from his New York office concerning the memoirs and he has to admit that Mrs. Porter has left him in the dark. Later he meets the princess, who is in the room next to his, and Nora drops by to lend him one of the cars attached to the *château*. His conversations with these two women buoy him up a bit, so that Jackson decides to relax and enjoy his stay in spite of Mrs. Porter. The following evening he takes Nora out to dinner and learns about her unhappy marriage as well as her tension with the old woman. He also develops his relationship with the princess by using the car to transport her between the hotel and the marquis's *château*. From her he learns more of Mrs. Porter's past, including the fact that her mother was a poor governess before her marriage. Both of the "good" women are providing Jackson with insights which he will ultimately add up into a truer picture of Mrs. Porter than he possessed at the novel's opening.

A day later Mrs. Porter invites him over to tea once more, and then reveals that she is finishing her memoirs. She makes this revelation in the midst of chastising Jackson for his attentions to Nora, her point being that she has sacrificed love for principle, and that he must do the same thing. Jackson, still full of American impulsiveness, refuses her advice and admits that he is falling in love with Nora. That evening he again takes the girl to dinner and tells her as much. Her response is somewhat ambivalent; clearly she feels affection for Jackson, but she also knows that she has responsibilities to her husband, no matter how weak he may be. During the evening they meet the princess, who gives their union her blessing, again in contrast with Mrs. Porter.

The old lady has a dramatic stratagem prepared to thwart Jackson's attentions to Nora; she gives a large cocktail party, inviting all of the characters and several outsiders, such as Oliver Winyard, and then springs Charles Marsh on them. Charles is too weak to handle the situation, and gets disgustingly drunk, a problem which Mrs. Porter blames on Nora and Jackson. Winyard and Philip Lenox revolt against her, placing the blame on her own domination of the young man. In fact the performance backfires, for not only does her lover turn against her, but Nora runs off to sleep with Jackson. He, of course, asks her to marry him, and the typical Basso happy ending seems to be shaping up.

However, Charles, now despondent about the ugliness at the party and the loss of Nora's love, tries to commit suicide, and Nora goes back to him. Mrs. Porter again accuses the lovers of trying to destroy her nephew, taking none of the blame on herself. Nora recognizes the unfairness of the charge, but she also realizes that if Charles is left with his aunt he will be destroyed. Jackson struggles to win Nora back, producing evidence from the princess, Spike Carruthers, and Philip Lenox that Mrs. Porter is a hypocrite and that Charles's attempted suicide might have been an accident, as he was drunk at the time. Still, Nora won't give up her resolve to stay with Charles if he will break with Mrs. Porter. When he elects to go to Australia with Philip Lenox, Nora tells Jackson that she must go, too. At the conclusion Jackson is left alone, traveling back to America, a wiser human being than when he left.

What he has learned is the Jamesian lesson that the New World is fallen as well as the Old, that the American Adam must experience this fall in order truly to discover his mature place in life. This is the same lesson which Henry James taught Christopher Newman in *The American* a generation earlier. It is a recurring theme in American literature, beginning with Cooper and Hawthorne, extending to James and Twain, and finally on to Faulkner and Hemingway. Basso, in *The Greenroom*, asserts his connection with the mainstream of American fiction, not just the Southern Renaissance. Though it is not a great novel, or a perfect one, *The Greenroom* is a well-conceived, well-crafted, well-written book, perhaps the best single work Basso created.

It makes *A Touch of the Dragon* doubly interesting that the only work in the Basso canon which it closely resembles proves perhaps his poorest novel. Again the chronological placement in the canon is of extreme importance in explaining *A Touch of the Dragon* (1964).

II A Touch of the Dragon

Basso enjoyed the success of the two Pompey's Head novels between the creation of his two novels centered on women characters. Though both Pompey's Head books were skillful productions connected with the whole Basso canon, they both tended toward commercial writing aimed at the best-seller lists and the movies. Unfortunately, Basso did not write the projected third volume of his trilogy about Pompey's Head during Reconstruction; instead he worked on an unfinished novel about Tahiti and then popularized *The Greenroom*, creating in *A Touch of the Dragon* a smooth little narrative in the manner of O'Hara, Marquand, or Cozzens. Certainly, much of the novel's weakness must be excused by Basso's declining health as he wrote the book; the author died only a few months after its publication.

Like *The Greenroom*, *A Touch of the Dragon* is set almost entirely outside of the South (one party is held in the Virginia suburbs of Washington), and it presents no important Southern characters; even the Basso protagonist is a Midwesterner. Unlike the earlier book, Basso is not moved to new developments by these changes; rather he seems to be constrained by settings and characters that he does not really know or understand. The setting is essentially the upper-middle-class world of an unnamed Midwestern city, which seems a good deal like Kansas City. Even when Basso changes the scene to New York, Virginia, or a Caribbean isle he still takes the same characters along, creating essentially the same setting. Of course, this setting is rather inherently dull, and Basso does little to liven it up. He has no eye for the details or ear for the dialogue. His Southern scenes, particularly Pompey's Head, are colorful in themselves and well rendered through long and loving observation. The Midwestern setting in *A Touch of the Dragon* seems merely a place to set the story.

This weakness extends to the depiction of character. The protagonist is once again the typical Basso hero, though here he is a non-Southerner. Sebastian Venables bears an interesting (and rather Southern) name, but little else about his personality is interesting. He narrates his own story and that of his major antagonist, Edwina Deydier, the "dragon lady" of the title, in an arch, gossipy style which fits well the dullness of his matter. Although he seems to be telling the story in the present—in other words, the early 1960s—the narrative deals essentially with his life between the ages of twenty-five and forty, the usual age limits of the Basso protagonist. The major difficulty with this novel is that nothing really exciting happens to the protagonist, at least after a youthful fling with the merchant navy and novel writing. He holds several jobs, he marries twice, he observes Edwina Deydier over the years, and at age forty he is relatively settled. Yet this life is presented without inward turmoil or outward event. Sebastian Venables is simply not as well characterized or as engaging as the other Basso protagonists, including Rufus Jackson of *The Greenroom*.

Even more of a problem exists in Sebastian's female antagonist, Edwina Deydier. Mrs. Porter of *The Greenroom* was an intriguing, exciting character who demanded the attention of both the Basso observer and the reader; Rufus Jackson's encounter with that formidable lady necessarily became a turning point in his life. Edwina is cut from the same cloth; she is rich, beautiful, energetic, ambitious, and theatrical. Unfortunately, she is also vain, shallow, and rather silly. It is the silliness which really hurts the author's characterization. The dragon just doesn't turn out to be much of a monster. Rather, she proves only an irritating person; Sebastian dislikes her, the other characters dislike her, even the reader dislikes her. Yet nobody could hate her; she engenders no passionate feeling—love or hate—in any of the characters or in the reader. She is ultimately pretentious, boorish, and eccentric, but little more. The reader feels at the end of the novel as if he has been listening to family gossip delivered in some detail about a slightly strange third cousin; his immediate reflex is to yawn.

The problems of characterization are amplified by plotting also, as Basso provides almost no meaningful relationship between Sebastian and Edwina. No more than acquaintances throughout the novel, Sebastian does little more than endure her. He doesn't sympathize with her; he doesn't understand her; rather he only stands by clucking his tongue in disapproval as Edwina stumbles through her eccentric existence. Because if nothing much happens to Sebastian, neither does anything very exciting or monstrous occur in Edwina's life. She grows up rich and somewhat spoiled, writes columns for the local newspapers (affecting working-girl outfits), discovers leftist politics (and switches to peasant blouses), then drifts into the worlds of art and literature (varied costumes), marries a phony literary critic, and, after she divorces him, an alcoholic Englishman. Aside from being occasionally pushy, petty, and nasty (particularly to her mother and sister), Edwina does little that could be condemned in a moral sense. Edwina Deydier, finally, proves pretty dull, though occasionally amusing.

So are the other characters, as the reader is again presented with a fine collection of proper Basso heroines. The most notable, as well as the most typical, is Susan Venables, a fifth cousin of Sebastian's, as well as his second wife. Susan is the younger sister of Claudia Venables, who was Sebastian's original *entre* to the society of the Midwestern city, and who first introduced him to Edwina. The sisters are rather indistinguishable except that Claudia is a little cattier, and thus not a suitable mate for the Basso hero. Edwina also has a younger sister, Julia, who is all sweetness and light in contrast to her; she conveniently marries a Scottish lord and goes off with him to his Highland castle, where she has five children (in contrast to the childless Edwina). Finally, there is Janet Poynter, Sebastian's first wife, another product of the country-club set in the Midwestern city; unfortunately she is somewhat neurotic, and wanders off, after she has had a miscarriage, to Colorado and then to Switzerland. The pattern of Sebastian's marriages reminds the reader of *Wine of the Country;* the first wife is somehow deficient, the second nearly perfect. In this case, the heroine is at least divorced. Susan married the very military Cliff Burdette during the war; he too is from the upper crust of the Midwestern city, but the couple soon discovers that they have nothing else in common. Besides which, he drinks and "chases." Hence the divorce, which enables her to settle down with the more solid Sebastian. Claudia's husband is not only solid, but stolid; a dully literal-minded industrial designer. The novel's other men are similar business and professional types, except for Covington Leeds, Edwina's first husband. Leeds proves something of a caricature, but he is really the only interesting person in the novel. A literary critic of small talents, he has a great sense of fashion and opportunity and propels a few critical insights into a rather successful career, including a brief marriage to Edwina. The undoing of their marriage is developed in the "literary" plot of the novel, which involves the fashionable practice of "discovering" a minor American writer of the nineteenth century. This part of the novel seems more extraneous satire than well-integrated action, but it still proves the most interesting aspect of this book.

The narrative follows Sebastian's involvement with Edwina, such as it is, beginning with a recent view of her striding along Fifth Avenue in New York City. From here he hearkens back to their first meeting at a country-club dance in the Midwestern city, given to celebrate Edwina's "coming out." A few flashbacks establish the history of her family and its money, as well as of the Venables family and its money. Sebastian himself, who is then a young newspaperman, is also introduced. The whole second chapter is devoted to his experience in the merchant marine after he chucks reporting, his trip to the South American banana port of Porto Vacas, his subsequent adventures in bars and brothels (all rather tame, actually), and his return to New York, where he tries to write a novel about his experience. After the novel fails to win the publishers' attention he junks his literary career in favor of journalism, attaining a wire-service job in the Midwestern city. By this time Edwina is raising dogs (Russian wolfhounds), and she begins her literary career by writing a dog column in the local paper. Sebastian thus gets to know her better and to dislike her even more, especially when she starts to act as if she is a working journalist herself. She also affects a feeling for the proletariat, the masses and the "workers," convincing Sebastian that she is an utter phony. He is more taken with Janet Poynter, a pretty young socialite he met through Claudia. They marry at about the same time that Susan marries Cliff Burdette, and Julia Deydier weds her Scottish lord. Of course, only Julia's marriage lasts. Sebastian and Janet are divorced within two years, the split caused by her neurotic feelings of insufficiency after she loses their baby.

Edwina meanwhile accompanies her sister to Europe after the wedding, and she returns home convinced that she should be writing a political column, "A View from the Heartland," rather than her "doggy" effort. The newspaper's editor, Mr. Standish, disagrees, even though he is her uncle. Sebastian is present at their confrontation, and he is amazed at her disdain for the older man. Earlier he had seen her mistreat her own father, now long divorced from her mother, but her rough treatment of the mild Mr. Standish seems even stranger to his mind.

After his divorce Sebastian decides to leave the Midwestern city, and he takes a job with another Venables family business, a small publishing firm in New York which specializes in atlases and travel books. Shortly after he takes the job Pearl Harbor is bombed, and he joins Army Intelligence because of his language ability. Essentially, Sebastian does nothing during the war but live in London translating the comments of Free French aviators who are flying reconnaissance missions over France. When he returns home, he visits the Midwestern city, discovers that Susan is divorced, and quickly marries her. They live in New York rather uneventfully for several years until some distant cousins invite them for a stay in Virginia. Here they run across Edwina, who has married Covington Leeds and moved to suburban Virginia.

Leeds is interested in meeting Susan's cousins, the Peales, because of his discovery of Gervase Peale, a generally forgotten late-nineteenth-century novelist. Peale had been a small-town lawyer in Virginia until middle age, when he suddenly bolted from the "genteel" tradition, establishing himself in a primitive paradise on Whaleman Island in the Caribbean. Here he lived a life of solitude, and wrote one novel, a minor classic of erotica called *The Daughters of Aphrodite*. Like Melville, Peale was ignored and forgotten by the twentieth century, at least until Covington Leeds discovers him. The modish Leeds is always on the lookout for new literary territory to stake out, and he strikes a gold mine in Gervase Peale. For Leeds the writer's appeal is not so much in his one novel as in his life-style; he sees Peale as an early-day sexual revolutionary, a forerunner of Gauguin and D. H. Lawrence. For a couple of years Leeds rides high on the strength of Peale's reputation, appearing on television as a sexual spokesman for a new generation, editing a new edition of Peale's work, and writing a critical study of Peale. Edwina even provides the money to buy Peale's old home on Whaleman Island and to underwrite a pictorial volume on "the island world of Gervase Peale."

Meanwhile, Sebastian has been plodding along in New York, watching the exploitation of Gervase Peale with a skeptical interest. Clearly Venables represents Basso's own view of literary criticism as practiced in the United States; his ultimate judgment is that Leeds sells "Snake Oil." Events prove him right. Another critic, an assistant professor at a small college in the Rocky Mountain states, decides to research Peale, and he discovers letters which prove Peale was a prude in life, if not in literature. Actually, all of Peale's erotic writing describes the amatory adventures of his brother Oscar, who stayed behind in Virginia practicing law. Leeds is, of course, torpedoed by this new discovery; Edwina becomes so enraged that she chases him back to New York and files for a divorce.

The Venableses come in on this climax of Edwina's literary development, because they are at that moment engaged in writing a *Guide to the West Indies* for their publishing company, and they decide to spend a week on Whaleman Island in company with Claudia and Charles Shattuck. What Basso seems to be saying is that Sebastian's *Guide* is a more realistic and valuable book than Leeds's *Pilgrimage of Gervase Peale.* After all, Sebastian did write a novel about the Caribbean himself. After the Gervase Peale bombshell explodes, they all try to be nice to Edwina, who will have none of it. Instead she plays in a tennis tournament against poor Mrs. Chichester, another island resident who has a heart murmur. During the match Mrs. Chichester's heart gives out on her, and the reader sees what a terrible person Edwina really can be. Of course, the judicious reader wants to ask why a woman with a heart murmur was playing in a tennis tournament in the first place. The author never fills the reader in on this point; instead he has Edwina marry the bereaved husband, the alcoholic Mr. Chichester. Now, with her money and her respectable, though weak, British husband, Edwina can go on to new sillinesses, or at least Sebastian so suspects when he sees her striding down Fifth Avenue. The novel ends when it comes back to this point; Sebastian and Susan have had a child and live happily ever after.

As even a short discussion demonstrates, *A Touch of the Dragon* is not a strong novel. The central characters are weak, and, what is worse, pretty dull. The plot provides no real action, adventure, or even antagonism. The theme seems simplistic; something like too much money can be bad for a person's development. The novel, particularly in view of its opening sentence, seems to hearken back through O'Hara to Fitzgerald and his story "The Rich Boy."[2] A comparison of this novel about a silly rich girl and Fitzgerald's complex fiction about the slow disintegration of Anson Hunter shows the weakness of Basso's effort. Perhaps he should have heeded the famous admonition which opens the Fitzgerald story: "Begin with an individual, and before you know it you have created a type; begin with a type, and you find you have created—nothing." Basso seems to have wanted to create a type; instead he wound up with a real nothing in Edwina Deydier, and, unfortunately, little more in Sebastian Venables. Their lack of life leaves the novel hollow, except for a few witty observations about the literary scene. *A Touch of the Dragon* thus proves the weakest of Basso's novels, though its weakness can be excused by the writer's declining health.

CHAPTER 6

The Pompey's Head Novels

BASSO told an interviewer that Pompey's Head, South Carolina, was conceived on a spring evening in Savannah, Georgia, a city which served as one model for the fictional locale.[1] Other models included New Orleans, Charleston, and Beaufort, South Carolina; in fact, Basso said that Pompey's Head would be located at Beaufort, if Beaufort were not there already. The Bassos had lived briefly in Beaufort during the 1930s, and it seems in general configuration much like the fictional Pompey's Head.[2] Basso had returned to Savannah and the Georgia coast in 1951, researching an article for *Holiday* magazine which appeared the following year.[3] Excited by his return to the heady world of the Southern coastal country which he had described in *Wine of the Country*, Basso decided to do another novel about the area. His novel would be about a specific place, Pompey's Head; he immediately wrote a ten-page description and history of the town, and even drew a map. The map reminds the reader of Faulkner's famous map of Yoknapatawpha County, based on his home county in Mississippi; Basso's "little postage stamp of soil," though not as richly populated, proves almost as fascinating.

After writing his description, he produced a novel concerned with a man of forty returning home to the South — *The View From Pompey's Head*. After it was published, Basso commented on further plans for Pompey's Head.

What I'd like to do is take the families of 1950 and go back to 1860. Then I'd do a third book on Reconstruction, when Anson Page's grandfather came down from New Hampshire. A sort of social history of the South done in the form of novels and about people.[4]

The novel of the Civil War became his next book, *The Light Infantry Ball*, published five years after *The View From*

106

Pompey's Head, in 1959. Unfortunately, Basso never wrote the third part of the projected trilogy, the novel about Reconstruction in Pompey's Head. The two novels he did finish are among his most interesting and most successful efforts, however, and they also proved to be his most popular.

I   The View From Pompey's Head

The View From Pompey's Head struck just the right balance between Basso's liberal Realism and the polished, popular narrative typified by John P. Marquand and James Gould Cozzens. The novel's popular success was spurred by the almost entirely enthusiastic reviewing in the major periodicals. Obviously written with an eye on the best-seller lists and the movies, the novel is also the logical development of Basso's fictional talents at this period of his career. It combines the two settings Basso knew best: the Southern small city and the publishing world of New York. It presents the typical Basso protagonist, now grown to be forty, in the person of Anson Page, and it employs the common theme of going home again, seen in so many of the novels, as Page travels back to his boyhood home. Basso's style, imagery, and symbolism are also refined from earlier novels. *The View From Pompey's Head* proves to be a refined, well-written, well-polished version of the typical Basso novel; it was his most popular novel, and perhaps his best overall effort.

In an enthusiastic review which appeared in the *New York Herald Tribune,* Coleman Rosenberger characterized *The View From Pompey's Head* in terms of three separate "novels" within its structure: the novel of character, the novel of suspense, and the novel of ideas; Mr. Rosenberger attributed the book's success to Basso's successful intertwining of the three forms.[5] This concept proves a useful one for critical discussion. The "novel of character" considers the development of Anson Page, forty-year-old successful New York lawyer originally from Pompey's Head. Page is older and more settled than the other Basso protagonists, but at the "dangerous" age of forty he must once more flirt with the attractions of the South before settling into his Northern career and marriage. The impetus for his first trip to "Old Pompey's" in fifteen years provides the suspense novel plot. A respected publishing company, long-time clients of Page's law firm, is caught in the middle of a potentially embarrassing situation; one of its most respected editors, now dead, has been accused of embezzling over $20,000 from the royalties of the company's prize property, the novelist Garvin Wales. Wales is now living on a coastal island near Pompey's Head, and Page is sent down to visit him in an attempt to clear up the mystery of the missing money, which seems to have been taken with Wales's permission. The realizations created by the trip back home and the solution of the Wales mystery emphasize Basso's theme in the novel—the dead weight of tradition which crushes the Southern spirit. This curse of the past weighing on the present has been a theme in other novels, but here it is most clearly articulated through the device of Page's observations and his book *The Shinto Tradition of the South.* Thus Basso is able successfully to combine his typical forms, "the novel of character" and "the novel of ideas," with the popular novel of suspense to create a product both critically and commercially successful.

Anson "Sonny" Page at forty appears to be well settled in all his vocations: family man, lawyer, and writer. Yet, in the spring of his fortieth year, he is strangely restless, restless in anticipation of spring, certainly; he appears in the early chapters complaining about the New York winter and reminiscing about the early spring of South Carolina. Yet it is more than spring fever bothering Page. He is at a point in life where he must make his adjustments in a rather permanent way, and he wonders if this life in New York is indeed what he wants. His life is circumscribed by the apartment and the office, by his career and his family. Both are basically attractive packages, but natural human doubts assail him at forty. Is this all there is?

He is a junior partner in the prestigious law firm of Roberts, Guthrie, Barlowe, and Paul, a position which he has worked hard to attain, and of which he is justly proud. His job pays very well, well enough to support a comfortable life-style in an East Seventies apartment; it provides status and identity; it even challenges him intellectually. One of the interesting aspects of his work involves the firm's clients, the giants of the publishing industry. Page has worked with the leading publishers and editors in New York, and he has even written and published his book with the encouragement of John Duncan, Sr., the president of Duncan and Company. Yet, for all his success, Page is feeling the pressure of the New York rat race. His law partners are dull suburban types, bent only on material success, and his boss, Mr. Barlowe, is something of an office tyrant. Page had once hoped to be an historian, to sit back and contemplate the meaning of life in a way which is impossible as a New York lawyer.

His home life is also rewarding, yet somehow deficient in Midwesterner and the niece of a U.S. senator. She is a bright, capable, attractive person—in short, the typical Basso heroine who should help the hero to live happily ever after. Anson is happy with Meg and their two children, Debby, seven, and Patrick, six. Meg has proved a good mother, much concerned with progressive education and the latest theories of child-rearing. In fact, she labors to keep up with the latest theories of everything; thus she is the typical New Yorker. Page respects all this in his wife, but after a dozen years of marriage he hearkens back to the passionate loves of his youth and wonders if love shouldn't hold more excitement than his seems to possess at the present.

All of Anson's vague dissatisfactions with his life in New York begin to focus on a comparison with Pompey's Head. He even talks about buying a farm in Connecticut or summer place in South Carolina to get away from the urban pressures of the city. Naturally enough, Pompey's Head become a symbol for him, a symbol of Edenic innocence and youthful exuberance. Pompey's Head represents what he was as a young man, and Anson yearns for this identity once again in the face of advancing middle age and his middle-class dissatisfactions.

Therefore his return to Pompey's Head is really a return to his youth, to his personal past in an attempt to understand what he was and what he has become. Basso utilizes a great deal of flashback to dramatize events of Anson's youth, his days as "Sonny" Page, an obviously symbolic nickname. These events clearly demonstrate that Pompey's Head is and was no earthly paradise; rather, it is the fallen Eden of the South, where the dead hand of the past strangles the vitality of the present. All of Page's recollections finally dramatize the theme of Southern Shintoism, an ancestor worship much different from the Oriental tradition, as Basso is careful to point out, because this false religion distorts the human reality of both the ancestors and the worshipers.

Some of "Sonny" Page's earliest reminiscence has to do with

his knowledge of Southern history. The town of Pompey's Head received its strange name when the first colonial governor remarked on the resemblance of the jutting bluff above the Cassava River to a man's head; in the classical spirit of 1720 he named the head for a noble character. The town supported the rebel cause during the Revolutionary War, raising the famous Light Infantry Regiment to battle for freedom. During the years before the Civil War, Pompey's Head rivaled Charleston and Savannah as a port; tons of cotton came down the Cassava to the Tidewater. During the war, the port was blockaded and much of the city destroyed by Union forces in 1865. Like its sister cities, Pompey's Head never quite regained its antebellum prosperity or importance, though it did have a spirit of growth when the railroad arrived in 1886. It was at about this time that Anson's grandfather, David Page, was making his mark as a hardware distributor, after emigrating from New Hampshire in the 1870s.

Sonny Page grew up in Pompey's Head during the years 1911 to 1936, when the city had once again become a small, sleepy port and distribution center. His grandfather's business had dwindled to the hardware store which his father operated, and Sonny was raised in middle-class circumstances. In a material way, he did not live differently from the rest of the town, for there was little of the old money left, especially during the Depression. But Sonny, with his carpetbagger grandfather, lacked "ancestors"; his mother's family was from the Piedmont, a yeoman stock which produced only cotton farmers and Baptist preachers. Sonny thus fell victim to the snobbery of the Pettibones and the Blackfords, while he in turn snobbed it over the rednecks and the Irish in a small way. None of this was too important to Sonny, who spent a rather idyllic youth, hunting and fishing with his friend Wyeth Blackford, studying local history and law at the state university.

After graduating with a law degree in 1934, Sonny returned to practice in Pompey's Head for two years, before leaving for New York. It was during this period that Sonny Page's social position becomes of the utmost importance. Like the typical Basso protagonist Sonny is sorting out his adult life, choosing a career and a wife. He sees himself as a successful lawyer with the local firm of Garrick and Garrick, yet one bringing some sense of racial justice to Pompey's Head, as he has picked up a liberal ideology at the state university. His interest in local history will be indulged through writing a column on the subject for the Pompey's Head newspaper. As a partner he chooses Kit Robbins, a very pretty girl from a newly rich family; and after courting through college they are engaged.

At this point Sonny's irascible father further alienates the community by encouraging a black man to bring suit against the venerable Mr. Pettibone, who had knocked the black through Page's store window for a fancied insult. The Pages, recalling the Barondess family in *Courthouse Square*, have always been suspect for their Northern-background liberal attitude, and now the town turns completely against them. A further complication for Sonny is the fact that the only witness, one who corroborates the Negro's story, is Midge Higgins, an Irish girl from the Channel Section, who was once sweet on Sonny. The Robbinses are worried about their social status and Kit is jealous; soon the engagement is broken, and Sonny is left brokenhearted. He then has a brief affair with Midge and a flirtation witht the Blackford's teenaged daughter, Dinah, before running off to New York, where he builds a new career and finds a new love.

Fifteen years later, in 1951, Anson Page returns to Pompey's Head, ostensibly to interview the novelist Garvin Wales, but in a more personal sense to see what he might have become if he had stayed in South Carolina. The novel opens with Page being called to leave his Pullman compartment as the train approaches Pompey's Head at the ungodly hour of 5:46 A.M. He recognizes the porter as an old-time resident of Pompey's Head, and he asks about the town, receiving the information that several of the blacks he knew as a boy have moved North. At the end of the novel, Anson reboards the same car, and the same porter asks him how he found the town. Page replies that nothing has changed. This is the major revelation of his return home; those who have not moved away are still the same, still slaves to the Shintoist tradition and the events of the dim past.

Some have moved, including Kit Robbins, who married well and lives on Chicago's North Shore, and Tooker McElroy, Sonny's boyhood black friend who has migrated to Detroit and the auto plants. But almost all the others have become what was expected of them. His other hunting companion, Wyeth Blackford, though the scion of one of Pompey's oldest families, has become the caretaker of the local fish and gun club. Sam Garrick, his youthful rival, has developed into a small-town, small-time shyster; Olive Darden, the local girl he married, suffers the typical sick headaches. One small surprise is that Mico Higgins, the tough younger brother of Midge Higgins, has developed into the town's richest citizen, as the president of a multi-industry conglomerate which he built from the ground up.

More surprising to Anson, who always respected Mico's ambition and ability, is the Channel boy's marriage to Dinah Blackford, Wyeth's younger sister. When he meets Dinah, she confesses her old crush on him and admits that she married Mico on the rebound, knowing that he had the ambition to restore the family fortunes. Anson also meets Midge, his onetime lover, who has married Bill Dillon, another Channel boy without Mico's success drive. Both women are still vital and attractive, but both demonstrate in their marriages the restraints of small-town life. Neither is happy or fulfilled, because they have married to fulfill the expectations of the community; Dinah to restore Mulberry, the Blackford plantation, and Midge to stay in her place as Channel Irish. Their reaction to Anson's return is also governed by class considerations; Midge is still attracted to him, but she has made her place in life and refuses to leave it. Dinah, in contrast, sees his visit as a chance to rekindle the old flame, and they have a brief, passionate affair.

It is this affair which most completely demonstrates to Anson the adolescence of his return to the past. Dinah may be beautiful, passionate, and redolent of his personal past in Pompey's Head, but she also proves willful, shallow, and a slave to her own past. Clearly their affair has nowhere to go in the future, which Anson would rather spend with Meg in New York.

At the same time he is receiving this lesson in terms of his marriage, he also learns another one in terms of his career. Shortly after he arrives at the Marlborough Hotel, he buys a guidebook to Pompey's Head published by the local historical association. The book makes more interesting reading over his breakfast than the local paper, but Anson soon realizes that this would have been the book he wrote if he had stayed in South Carolina. His *Shinto Tradition of the South* could only have been written from the detached perspective of the North, with its more cosmopolitan point of view.

More importantly, he learns that even the best and most talented Southern writers are constrained by their heritage as he unravels the mystery of Garvin Wales. Born in Alabama, Wales had wandered the world, finally turning up as a soldier on the Mexican border in 1916 at about the age of thirty. Here he met Phillip Greene, then a young man just out of Harvard. The two soldiers formed a friendship, and Greene encouraged Wales to write his first novel. The book, entitled *Cenotaph,* was a sensational best-seller, its sales spurred by recognition of Wales's talents and of the novel's frank sexuality. From this point Wales had written a dozen fine books, all edited by Greene and published by Duncan and Company. (The book also seems something of the *roman a clef* as Wales seems compounded from O'Neill, Faulkner, and Hemingway, while Greene seems modeled on Max Perkins and Saxe Commins.) Shortly after the First World War, in which Wales served as a flyer, he married Lucy Deveraux, daughter of an old-line South Carolina family who was trying to make a career on Broadway. Later she gave up her career to follow Wales around the world as he sought inspiration and solitude to write his novels, novels which built him the reputation as America's greatest writer. In his old age Wales and his wife have retired to Tamburlane Island off the South Carolina Coast near Pompey's Head. As Wales sank into physical blindness and ill health, Lucy began to do more and more of his business for him, finally driving off most of his old friends, including Phillip Greene.

Now, in 1951, Lucy Wales has discovered that $20,000 of her husband's royalties have been systematically removed from his account by Phillip Greene, who died a few years earlier. John Duncan believes that Greene could have easily explained the situation, which he feels must have been countenanced by Wales. In the course of his investigation into the missing money, Anson discovers a folder of Greene's checks corresponding exactly to the amounts taken from Wales's account and made out to one Anna Jones. He assumes that the woman was one of Wales's mistresses, perhaps a black woman from her name and address, supported in this way to keep Lucy from knowing about her. Wales will have to admit this, however, or Duncan and Company will be forced to make up the money as these suppositions would not stand up in court.

Both Wales and his wife at first refuse to cooperate with him, but by the end of the novel Anson has found out Wales's secret. Anna Jones was a mulatto woman, and she was not Wales's mistress but his mother. Wales is terrified that Lucy will find this fact out and leave him alone in his old age. This knowledge, which is discovered through a detection process much like a good mystery story, puts Anson Page in a difficult position. He does not want to hurt Wales, but he cannot betray his client either. Finally, he chooses the professional attitude that his client is not going to spend $20,000 to support Pompey's Head's views on race and marriage. Page forces Wales to face up to his situation, and he faces up to his own by breaking off the affair with Dinah and leaving on the first train for New York.

This "novel of suspense" within the overall framework of the book is well handled both as a mystery story and as a component of Basso's narrative. Wales is one of his most memorable characterizations, and Lucy is one of his successful older women, much like Mrs. Porter of *The Greenroom*. Most importantly, this plot underlines the same themes recognized in the "novel of character," the narrative of Anson Page's growth and development. Even a Southerner as cosmopolitan in his nature as Garvin Wales succumbs to the slavery of tradition when he returns to the South. If even a great writer can finally be choked by the dead hand of the past, Anson concludes that no one could survive the crushing weight of the past in Pompey's Head. Thus the "novel of ideas" emerges naturally from his narrative materials, and combining with the stories of Anson Page, Garvin Wales, and the other characters creates one of Basso's best novels, a book which certainly deserved the popular success it won.

II   The Light Infantry Ball

In the second of the Pompey's Head novels, *The Light Infantry Ball* (1959), Basso fulfilled his promise to trace the families of 1951 back to 1861. The second novel covers the years 1861 to 1865, with a few flashbacks to earlier times, and it involves the ancestors of many characters who appear in *The View From Pompey's Head*. The specific connections of names and places are not as important, however, as the thematic parallelism between the two books; in essence, *The Light Infantry Ball* explains the strangle hold of the past on the present, the major theme of the earlier book. Basso's protagonist, John Bottomley, proves to be as crippled by tradition as many of the modern residents of Pompey's Head, though the novel holds out hope that, like other Basso heroes—Anson Page, for example—he will develop a mature vision better than the typical "viewpoint" of that community. Thus *The Light Infantry Ball* places the typical Basso protagonist in a different historical context, but one which evolves similar themes and ideas through the narrative line. Basically, the novel succeeds well; Basso's careful historical research, incisive character portrayals and complex themes all combine to create a book much better than the usual "historical novel." At the same time, the author's difficulties with plot, particularly the romance plots, limit his success in the book, finally placing it a cut below *The View From Pompey's Head*.

Much like the earlier novel about Pompey's Head, *The Light Infantry Ball* can be viewed as several different types of novel: the historical novel, the novel of character, the novel of ideas, and even the novel of detection. Probably Basso is most successful in the historical aspects of the novel. He had written well of the past as background to the present South in other novels, and had successfully dramatized the Civil War period in the flashbacks of *Cinnamon Seed*. Certainly *The Light Infantry Ball* is no moonlight-and-magnolias romance. The author was a lifelong student of Southern history, and in the novel he employed his special knowledge to good effect, writing one of the most realistic fictional portraits of the Civil War in Southern literature. Basso's careful creation of the Pompey's Head setting insures that his details are accurate, but more importantly, unlike many historical novels, the details are formed into a truthful vision of the spirit of the time.

According to the vision of this novel, that spirit was not as simplistic or as homogeneous as usually is assumed; in fact, Basso's Civil War period seems rather modern in its anxieties, frustrations, and failures. This realization is dramatized by presenting the diversity of Southern character and opinion during the era. The central personality, John Bottomley, recalls David Barondess, the dissenting plantation owner mentioned in *Courthouse Square;* he questions the morality of slavery, opposes the policy of secession, and doubts that the South could win the war. At the opposite end of the ideological spectrum stands Ules Monckton, a "fire-eater," ambitious for personal advancement, who defends slavery as a moral institution, leads the attack on federal outposts in South Carolina, and refuses to surrender at the end of hostilities. Bottomley and Monckton are opposed throughout the book as protagonist and antagonist, and, finally, the novel demonstrates the destructive effect of "fire-eating" fanaticism on Southern culture. Both characters are real historical types; Monckton might well be based on Robert B. Rhett or Edward Ruffin, noted Southern fanatics, though his military career is to some extent based on Basso's earlier biographical subject, General P. G. T. Beauregard. Between these two character extremes are gathered a myriad of personalities, some strong, some weak; some patriotic, some venal; some agonized by their situation, others hardly aware of it.

All of these characters are gathered around John Bottomley, the novel's protagonist and central intelligence. Bottomley proves a typical Basso protagonist; at the opening of the novel in 1861 he is just thirty years old, still unmarried, and still unsettled in a career. He is also a sensitive, intelligent, sympathetic personality, with a good deal more liberal insight into the world around him than the other members of the Planter society. The Bottomleys are one of the oldest and wealthiest families in the area, as their ancestor, Christian Bottomley, arrived with Governor Alwyn and the original group of settlers and soon established Deerskin Plantation. He acquired this property by marrying an Indian princess and taking it as a dowry. Over the years the Bottomleys married no other Indians, but they continued to acquire valuable properties. John's ancestors also led the Light Infantry into battle during the Revolution, and his father, Corwin, was elected governor of the state.

The family had the money to send John off for his education at Princeton, where his skepticism about the views and values of Pompey's Head was compounded by the instruction of his favorite teacher, the abolitionist Professor Sedgewick. John, in fact, decided to become an architect, after first flirting with authorship as a career. Two reversals destroyed his plans, however, and rendered him almost completely passive about his future. First, he declared himself to Clarissa Drew, a well-brought-up young lady of Philadelphia, who turned him down rather coldly. Immediately after his rejection his father suffered some financial reverses in building his big townhouse, Indigo, forcing John to drop out of school.

For a decade after returning home to Pompey's Head, John manages Deerskin Plantation, thirty miles up the Little River from the town. Here he lives completely isolated, working hard to keep the rice plantation profitable while reading, hunting, and drinking for his entertainment. During this decade, he makes only one real attempt at human contact; again he declares himself to a woman, Lydia Chadwick, his younger sister's schoolteacher. Lydia has her ambitious eye on the widowed Senator Stanhope, the father of another student, so she also rejects poor John. After this refusal and Lydia's subsequent marriage to the senator, John becomes even more of a recluse.

As the novel opens, the rapidly moving events of January 1861 are forcing him back into the mainstream of life in Pompey's Head. The South is on the verge of secession, with the firebrands, such as Ules Monckton, counseling an immediate attack against the federal positions. A personal crisis also threatens the Bottomleys; John's younger brother, Cameron, has disappeared. Cameron, who is twenty-five, has always been something of a problem to John; hotheaded and highliving, he has borrowed heavily from his older brother. Now John suspects that the young rake is in some serious trouble, serious enough to run out on his engagement to Kitty Williams, which was to have been announced at the Light Infantry Ball. Given annually on January 18, this social event celebrates the Battle of Little Pigeon Marsh, the occasion of the Light Infantry's greatest triumph. Corwin Bottomley, as ex-governor, is to be this year's grand marshall, and thus John is forced to attend. More problems ensue when his mother, always a neurotic, collapses completely when her younger son disappears.

At the ball, he is forced to make weak excuses for his brother, to dance with all the local belles, including the flirtatious Arabella Stanhope, the senator's daughter and Lydia's step-daughter, and to argue against the cause of secession. He finally enters into a very heated discussion with Ules Monckton which ends when the firebrand implies that John is not a true son of the South. The implications here are quite interesting; John's filial relationship to the South is similar to that with his parents. He loves and respects his family and his homeland, and, though reserving the right to question their conduct, he is steadfastly loyal to them. After all, when he was asked to come home and help the family he did not rebel and go off to be an architect in Europe.

In this sense, John Bottomley, though still the Basso pro-tagonist in broad outline, is more the man of his day rather than of modern times. When challenged in his love of the South, he responds emotionally, insults Monckton, and is in turn challenged to a duel. What is more, his adherence to tradition forces him to go through with the fight, at the risk of his life, because it is the thing which a Southern gentleman would do. John fires into the air, but Monckton tries to hit his opponent, wounding him in the elbow. Even as he is wounded, John realizes that the argument, the fight, and the wound itself have involved him in the Southern cause to such an extent that he will have to stand with the South, though he disagrees with the Southern moral position. The wound cripples John's arm for life, but it is more important as a symbol of the crippling effect of the Southern tradition on the personality when uncritically accepted.

The ball and the duel, along with a good deal of flashback to explain their background, take up Parts One and Two of the novel, about 140 pages of text. Parts Three and Four begin a few weeks after the duel and are essentially concerned with the mystery of Cameron's disappearance. It takes John a few weeks to recover sufficiently from his serious wound to begin a more thorough search for Cameron. In the meantime, these difficulties are weighing heavily on the Bottomley family. Mrs. Bottomley is becoming more and more unstable, now believing, in the wake of many "Yankee spy" stories, that the family servants are going to burn the house down around them. Mr. Bottomley, troubled by his wife's collapse, also becomes ill, and John, barely recovered from his wound, has to take over the family business. His sister Missy does provide some help and stability, however, as John slowly unravels the mystery surrounding Cameron.

This part of the novel is essentially a mystery story, and it is presented in that form, with John receiving certain clues and using his increasing knowledge to solve the problem. As a separate novel within the novel this section is entertaining enough as narrative, but it finally has little connection with the main story and the main themes of the book. John discovers that Cameron had become infatuated with a beautiful Channel girl, Maria O'Connell, the daughter of an Irish immigrant family living in one of Corwin Bottomley's rental properties. While attempting to seduce her, he was confronted by her brother and forced to kill him in the ensuing fight. Now he has fled the country in fear of detection, aided by Albright, a Free Negro barber, who in reality is Corwin Bottomley's half brother and John and

Cameron's uncle. This revelation about Cameron is interesting
enough in itself, but it is too long in coming and somewhat beside
the point. It could be argued that Cameron's actions demonstrate
the corruption of the Southern tradition, the young man given
over to seduction and violence, but the connections are too
vague and general to be really meaningful.

While John has been seeking the solution to this mystery,
events from the other plot also have been marching onward. Ules
Monckton has raised a regiment and marched against the forts on
the estuary of the Cassava River, thus accelerating the onset of
the war. Soon Fort Sumter is also attacked and South Carolina
secedes from the Union, quickly joined by the other Southern
states. Now everyone is drawn into war preparations and the
prodigal Cameron is forgotten. Corwin Bottomley has been
asked to join the new government, but his health has failed too
badly for any service. John is also excused from active duty
because of his crippled arm, so he joins the staff of Senator
Stanhope, who has been appointed Secretary of the Interior for
the new Confederate States government. Just as he prepares to
leave for Richmond, his mother dies in a final neurotic fit,
frightened to death of a black insurrection.

Part Five is set in Richmond during 1862, as the war is starting
to turn against the South. Once again Basso's scholarship is
impeccable, and the portrait of the nervous capital is especially
well drawn. In this section another mystery story, one more
interesting than Cameron's disappearance, is also developing.
John's particular job is keeping track of all the cotton processed
throughout the South. This obviously is an enormous task, and a
very difficult one, because much cotton-smuggling is going on.
With the Northern blockade, cotton has soared from ten cents to
a dollar a pound in Europe, and fortunes are being made by
privateers who can get the cotton out of the South. In the midst
of general confusion, incompetence, and indifference, John and
one of his underlings named Rawlins discover that huge amounts
of cotton are being smuggled out of New Orleans, evidently with
the protection of the agent there, who turns out to be Lydia
Stanhope's cousin. John suspects that Lydia and the senator may
be in on this fraud, so he is uncertain about his course of action.
Over the years he has kept a romantic ache for Lydia, and now
he has to face up to the truth about her—that she is completely
venal and self-serving. Lydia tries to seduce him from his duty,

but now his course is clear to him. As he moves to reveal the
scandal, the senator repays the government for the lost cotton
and then commits suicide, a victim of Lydia's ambitions.

Several other developments occur while John is unraveling the
mystery of the missing cotton. Cameron has surfaced again,
broke and despondent, evidently disintegrating without his
family identity to preserve him. Arabella Stanhope and John are
thrown together by the crisis in the Stanhope family, and they
soon recognize that they are in love. General Ules Monckton has
also come to Richmond, counseling an offensive war against the
North, and has been "exiled" off to the relatively isolated
Western theater of the war. Finally, John is so sickened by the
corruption of the home front that he volunteers for combat duty
in spite of his crippled arm.

Part Six, the conclusion of the novel, takes place in the spring
of 1865. John has fought his way through all the major campaigns
on the Virginia front, demonstrating considerable valor and
leadership qualities. He has taken time away from the war only
to marry Arabella, at the same time that his sister Missy weds
Gordon Carpenter. Now he is part of a detachment under
General Monckton sent to oppose Sherman's march through
South Carolina; their force has been beaten badly near
Columbia, retreating toward Pompey's Head. Quite obviously
the end of the war is near, and John only hopes that he can
preserve Pompey's Head from destruction until the surrender
takes place. Monckton fanatically refuses to surrender, even if
Lee does, and he proposes a scorched-earth and guerrilla
campaign to harass the Northern forces.

John and Monckton dramatically oppose each other once more
when the troops are rallied at Indigo, the Bottomley home. After
another debate, reminiscent of their argument at the Light
Infantry Ball, John tells Monckton that he will kill him this time if
he tries to burn the house. Missy and Arabella, who has been
living with her since her father's suicide, are in the house, and
they are defended by Albright, the mulatto uncle. In the ensuing
struggle, Monckton kills Albright and John wounds Monckton,
though he is unable to keep him from setting the house afire. The
blazing mansion becomes Monckton's funeral pyre, however, and
when he dies the spirit of the "fire-eaters" goes out of the troops,
who accept John's leadership. The symbolism is neat, if obvious;
Mrs. Bottomley had been afraid that the blacks would burn the

house, while John feared the Yankees, but it turns out that the Southern fanatic was responsible for the destruction of this symbol of the old order. From the burning house John has rescued only one object, the symbolic gold ceremonial cane which is carried by the Grand Marshall of the Light Infantry Ball. The novel concludes with Arabella observing that there will be another ball someday. Tradition lives on to become crippling again in future generations.

This conclusion, so obviously recalling *Gone With the Wind*, only serves to emphasize the plot difficulties of the novel. The settings of Pompey's Head and Richmond during the Civil War are carefully and successfully rendered. The central character, a typical Basso protagonist, provides interest as a thoughtful liberal opposed to the destructive drift of the South, incarnated in the person of his main antagonist, Ules Monckton. Other characters, such as Corwin Bottomley, Albright, and Clay Vincent, a hotheaded young soldier, are well drawn also. The opening of the war, the mystery of the disappearing cotton, and the collapse of the Confederacy are nicely handled sections of the plot.

Yet the novel flounders on its romance plots. The whole affair of Cameron Bottomley and the beautiful Irish girl is rather unbelievable, and certainly extraneous to the real development of the novel. John's rejection by the icy Lydia and his acceptance by the spirited Arabella are both right out of stock Southern romance; the two women are both incredible clichés: the destructive "bitch" and the supportive heroine. In his romantic actions John behaves, as one critic put it, "like a character played by Nelson Eddy in an operetta."[6] Their relationships are hackneyed, and, most importantly, they are not really a part of the real vision of the novel.

Thus, Basso's excursion into Southern history is only partially successful. The historical aspects of the novel are accurate and interesting, but the "historical-novel" aspects, particularly the local color and the romantic plot, are stereotyped and mechanical. One reviewer called the book "an adult Southern" in obvious comparison to the adult Western of the *High Noon* variety popular in the late 1950s.[7] The phrase is apt, because it catches the relationship of the book to literary traditions. *The Light Infantry Ball* is much better than one would expect a novel about the Civil War to be; it definitely has an "adult," realistic aspect.

On the other hand, it is caught up in the clichés and stereotypes of a literary tradition which almost dictate its failures. All in all, the novel seems good entertainment, which also provides some of the elements Basso handles well: the Southern setting, the central character, the readable style. It did sell very well, particularly on the strength of the author's previous performance in *The View From Pompey's Head.*

Finally, it is interesting to speculate about the projected but unwritten third volume of the trilogy, the book to be concerned with Reconstruction in Pompey's Head. It might have been the best of the three, as it would have gotten Basso into another historical setting, without involving him in the stereotypes of the Civil War story. Some of Faulkner's best writing concerns the Reconstruction period; perhaps Basso might also have done well with this period of Southern history. It is a shame that he did not work on this novel; rather, he worked on the unfinished Tahiti novel, and his final book was the previously discussed *A Touch of the Dragon,* one of his weakest efforts, which was published shortly before his death in 1964.

CHAPTER 7

The Short Stories

A S the earlier chapters of this study have stressed, Hamilton Basso is most important as a novelist of the Southern Renaissance, but, like most novelists, Basso occasionally tried his hand at the short story. Although he published only ten short stories during his long career, they are important for the critic of Basso's fiction because of their connections with the novels and their development of new matter and techniques. Also, the overall quality of this work proves as fine as anything in his novels. In fact, the novels often include self-contained pieces of narrative which seem almost like short stories; some examples are the Civil War stories in *Cinnamon Seed,* the story of the *Kala-azar* plague in *Days Before Lent,* and the hunting sequences in *Wine of the Country.* The last are especially close to Basso's best stories, which are concerned with both hunting and fishing. In view of his real success with the form, particularly in this later group of stories, and of his difficulties with plotting in the novel, it seems strange that Basso did not write more widely in the shorter forms. Probably the commercial difficulty of earning a living by selling short stories coupled with the short story's inadequacy for presenting larger social and philosophical ideas kept Basso from fuller development in this form.

Aside from some early unpublished pieces Basso's stories fall into three chronological groupings: two stories published in Eugene Jolas's *transition* in 1929 and 1933; two short sketches from 1935; and the six hunting and fishing stories which appeared in the *New Yorker* between 1944 and 1947.[1] As in the treatment of the novels, this chapter will take up the stories in chronological order, except where obvious affinities of material and theme make other pairings more practical, as in the paired stories of hunting and violence, fishing and initiation, and eccentric old sportsmen.

123

Basso's earliest published story, "I Can't Dance," appeared in
Eugene Jolas's *transition* for June 1929. In the April 1929 issue of
Jolas's influential journal, Basso had published a "Letter" from
New Orleans which despaired over the state of literature in
America. The tone of his report is somewhat sophomoric, almost
as if Tony Clezac, the protagonist of *Relics and Angels,* had
written it; lurid images of literary revolt against gentility climax
his report, reminding the reader of Tony's inflammatory speech
to the workers. The spirit of the "Letter" and the first novel also
pervades this first story, which forms part of a sheaf of "new"
works from the United States in Jolas's special "Revolution of the
Word" issue.

"I Can't Dance" proves to be rather stridently antigenteel,
though not revolutionary in either content or form. Its protagonist is Malcolm, a young white-collar worker in New Orleans.
Malcolm lives in a world of decaying gentility; his widowed
mother has been reduced to keeping a boardinghouse, and his
dreary office job barely keeps him in lunches and cigarettes. He
has recently become engaged to Katherine, a forthright though
dull young lady, who has received her moral training from the
Reverend Marcus of the Baptist Church. The images used to
depict the boardinghouse, the office, and Katherine all present a
picture of decay, sterility, and paralysis. The effects seem much
like those created by Joyce's stories in *Dubliners*, stories which
were widely influential on the development of the form in the
1920s, or those of Sherwood Anderson's stories in *Winesburg,
Ohio.*

Basso's narrative concerns one flicker of revolt on the part of
Malcolm, one desperate attempt at movement beyond the
paralyzing constrictions of genteel Southern life. Working late on
a hot summer night, Malcolm has listened in fascination as his
officemates spun tales of sexual adventures in the red-light
district of the city. Their stories correspond to his own fantasies:
". . . blazing panoramas of vice, gorgeous rooms where women
danced, and surrendered and were borne triumphantly away"
(128). In particular, Malcolm is fascinated by a coworker's
description of a lewd dance performed by two prostitutes in a
brothel. Inflamed by this image Malcolm sets out for the red-
light district—after a long battle with his puritanical conscience.

His "nighttown" is the notorious area of the cribs in the New
Orleans tenderloin. Women of the night beckon from every door,

calling out to him in husky voices. He tries to talk with Mabel, an experienced denizen of the cribs, but she has no time for anything beyond the basics of her business. Hilda, a younger, prettier girl, gives him the same brushoff. After suffering the derisive hoots of all the crib girls, Malcolm is finally accepted by a young black prostitute. After much talk, he offers her money to dance for him. Quickly shedding her shift, the girl hums a jazz tune and sways easily in the yellow light. But her dance is only an approximation of the abandon Malcolm has imagined, and the story ends with this ironic epiphany.

> "What's the matter" he said "Why don't you dance? Why don't you go ahead and dance?"
> The song she was singing died in her throat. The muscles of her legs and arms relaxed and were at ease. She looked at him and slowly backed toward the bed. He couldn't take his eyes from her.
> "I can't dance, Mister" she said "I ain't never danced before. I just can't dance." (132)

Thus Malcolm's one gesture toward rebellion and escape ends in sordid frustration. Altogether the story seems well conceived and well realized. There is a certain awkwardness about the Joycean epiphany attempted in the conclusion, but otherwise the characterization and the writing prove effective. Like *Relics and Angels*, the story seems influenced by the best writers of the era; unlike the first novel their influence is absorbed into Basso's own vision and unified in an aesthetically pleasing whole. "I Can't Dance" merited its inclusion with works by Gertrude Stein, Kay Boyle, and Erskine Caldwell in Jolas's "Revolution of the Word" issue of *transition*.

Basso's second story also was published in *transition*, some four years after his first effort; "Rain on Aspidistra" appeared in the February 1933 issue, one which included a continuation of James Joyce's "Work in Progress," later to become *Finnegans Wake*. "Rain on Aspidistra" proves entirely appropriate to this context; it is easily Basso's most uncharacteristic piece, a Joycean stream-of-consciousness conundrum transported to the mountains of Virginia. Though lacking the symmetrical mythic structuring and the verbal ingenuity of the Joycean work, Basso's story proves an interesting experiment, one much more successful than the other imitations of "Work in Progress" so common at that time in the avant-garde journals.

Published in 1932, the story presents in different form and style the subject matter and themes which were Basso's preoccupations of this moment when he was finishing the biography of General Beauregard and starting the novel which became *Cinnamon Seed*. Therefore, he was much concerned with Southern history and with the effect of the past on the present. The rain on the aspidistra provides the contemplative subject of the story which the writer-narrator-protagonist uses to descend below and then above the conscious level of his understanding. At first sinking into the passages and pools of his body, he is "suddenly in flight" (11), though the flight is into the unconscious mind where he can recall the visions of other times.

The sheer dark wall is eloquent and I detect familiar shapes and forms, young ambitions and determinations abandoned stillborn, caught floated in a seashapened rook in all their young and helpless suffering.
I remember the vortices of young designs, the river of skulls and blood, all the slithering fish opening their thorny mouths to murmer patriotic songs. (11)

His memory is also the racial memory of the South, his *patrias*, and he soon meets his major antagonist, the devil, in the form of a Dixie gentleman hissing an Alabama drawl. The protagonist cannot worship this false deity, so he makes war on the very "hinges" of Hell itself. The outcome is ambiguous, but the battle frees the narrator.

I am rejoicingly free but have lost all awareness of my former identity. I wander on the mountains, which I love, listening to the sound of the waterfalls. The sun sets, striking the rocks with bronze, and beyond the sun is the glacial purity of the sky. Little houstonias glow like starsplinters between the rocks of Carthaginian bronze. Somewhere a bird sings, dropping notes into the utter quiet and they resolve themselves into bright metaphors which fall into the rhododendrons with the sound of fragile bells. I pick them up and they are very beautiful and I put them by for a leaner time. (13)

Climbing farther in the mountain, the path becomes the stairway to his old attic (again the uncionscious mind), where he meets Jeb Stuart, the apotheosis of Southern gallantry. Stuart captures Grant, and the South triumphs in this dream vision of a glorified history.

Suddenly back on the mountain, the protagonist watches a wrinkled crone—half mountain woman, half classical fate—weaving "prosaic cloth" into beautiful artistic visions. Her peace in the mountains reminds him that he is of the lowlands, and soon he is beside the great river (the Jordan and the Mississippi), where he visits a Catholic service for the dead and then experiences a final apocalyptic vision.

> And now, while empty sound signifies thunder, the red clouds, pregnant with wine and blood, are ridden by all the Confederate Generals about the ring of stars, cavorting gayly with ribands of silver and blue until, outraged by the gutrumblingly graylord gray nothingness of his unctuous tone, they pour down the blessing of wine and good saints' blood that beat with eventual understanding upon the taut canvas of my mind. (14-15)

Again the Confederate generals are beatified, sanctified of the evil of the Alabamian devil (perhaps the despised Jefferson Davis), and they become the true priests of a cleansing sacrament. Both Baptism and Communion are suggested by the red clouds, as are drunkenness and war. Yet against the grayness, the genteel dullness of the Catholic priest, they pour down a vital blessing. Transfigured, the Confederate generals become the angels of the understanding which the protagonist will transform into art. The canvas of the final sentence probably recalls both the cloth of the old woman and the canvas of the painter. Basso would create his panoramic "canvas" of Southern history in *Cinnamon Seed* only a few years later, and certainly the surrealistic images of this story relate to that realistic achievement.

Although it is not a completely successful piece, "Rain on Aspidistra" certainly proves one of Basso's most interesting efforts. The story's surrealism sometimes gets out of control, and it does not seem an appropriate mode for Basso's characteristic social observations. Yet the poetic possibilities of the dream sequence, the intensely personal symbolism, and the rich imagery suggest qualities lacking in much of Basso's other writing. Perhaps in turning away from these experiments Basso limited his own possibilities, much as he did with the commercial conclusions of some of his novels. At the least, the student of Southern literature wishes that Basso had written more short stories such as "Rain on Aspidistra" where, beyond commercial restraints, he might have developed techniques which would have enriched his novels.

"Me and the Babe," a short sketch published in the *New Republic* in April of 1935, is undoubtedly Basso's slightest story, one which represents the less-interesting directions of Basso's talents. The story is set in New York, and like those parts of his novels set there — *Courthouse Square*, for example — the descriptions, the dialogue, and the actions do not quite ring true. "Me and the Babe" proves even more problematic because it is a sort of Hamilton Basso version of Damon Runyon.

The protagonist, a "hick" fresh from Franklin, Louisiana, walks Broadway observing the Runyonesque "smart boys" congregating around the dance halls and cigar stores. His friendly hellos are greeted by stares of disbelief. One evening, while watching the electronic news flashes on the Times building, the protagonist is accosted by one of these characters who wants to sell him a cut-rate watch. Our hero has no interest in the watch, but he engages the Broadway denizen in a conversation about Babe Ruth, who has just been traded from the Yankees to Boston. The character asserts a lifelong friendship with the Babe, and promises to introduce him when he plays in town. When the watch is still declined, the con man abandons the narrator for another mark.

The story works better in summary than in full telling. Because its viewpoint is the central character's and its action mainly a dialogue between the men, voice becomes very important. But Basso cannot do New York accents, and even his Franklin, Louisiana, native winds up sounding like bad Damon Runyon. For example:

> "I would have sworn you were the man who said he was going to buy my watch off of me."
> "No," I say. "You are mistaken. I have not promised to buy a watch off of no one."
> "That is too bad for you," he answers. "It is a very fine watch." (309)

Thus the characters emerge as little more than the stereotypes of the movie bit parts played by character actors. The action is also too slight to sustain any real interest.

The story's only real strength resides in the central conception. The linking of Babe Ruth to the Broadway character, and the paralleling of the watch deal and the baseball deal, provide an incisive revelation of the American character. The Babe, the "Man who Built Yankee Stadium" with his towering home runs, probably the greatest player the national pastime has ever known, was sold off by the Yankee management when his aging legs gave out on him. Basso neatly demonstrates that the baseball magnates, the guardians of the national heritage, are no more honest than the Broadway con man. The Great White Way has its own heart of darkness beneath the neon glitter.

The more palpable darkness at the heart of Hitler's Germany is the subject of a story published in the same month, "Fabulous Man," appearing in the prestigious *Scribner's Magazine*. Reminiscent of Wolfe's "I Have a Thing to Tell You," Basso's story concerns an American traveling in Germany who is initially attracted to the land and its people. A dramatic incident then reveals the dark and terrible things beneath the shining surfaces of a neurotic society. However, Basso's story suffers in comparison with Wolfe's because his characterization and plotting are the commonplaces of commercial fiction. Although the story seems well intentioned, it finally fails to become first-rate fiction.

A young American, a "Basso protagonist" type named David, is traveling in Germany with his mother. Against his will he is charmed by the storybook beauty of Bavaria and by the blonde beauty of a young woman, Freida. The two have climbed the mountain above her town to be alone and talk. Essentially the story consists of their dialogue, a dialogue which concerns two famous figures—Albert Einstein and Adolph Hitler. David is a recent Princeton graduate, and he mentions seeing Einstein on the campus after he was exiled from Germany. Freida replies that Einstein, like all Jews, is an enemy of Germany; *The Leader* has said so often. When David in turn attacks Hitler, Freida replies heatedly and runs off.

I think you must be a Jew yourself. There must be Jewish blood in your veins. I will have nothing to do with one who loves Jews. (218)

David is left alone to curse *The Leader* as "that bastard" (218).

The story works in the same general patterns as "Me and the Babe." Two characters engage in dialogue which centers on symbolic figures of their culture. Of course, "Fabulous Man" is much more serious in tone and intent, though both stories

demonstrate how the darker sides of human nature pervade a
culture. The difficulties of "Fabulous Man" also resemble those
of "Me and the Babe." The characterization is flat, as both David
and Freida are characters out of ladies' magazine fiction, and the
action is slight, at least in comparison with Wolfe's account of the
old Jews's arrest in "I Have a Thing to Tell You." As in the New
York tale, the detail and dialogue are not convincing. Thus like
much of his longer fiction, Basso's story "Fabulous Man" proves
ideologically laudable, but artistically deficient; it is good
propaganda but weak fiction.

These two little stories were the last Basso published until
1944, when he began a series of hunting and fishing stories in the
New Yorker. During this period the writer was working at the
New Yorker, living in Weston, Conn., and lying fallow between
novels. Undoubtedly the combination of a ready market for his
short pieces and the absence of a longer project encouraged
Basso to make his only substantial effort in the short-story form.
These hunting and fishing stories develop some of the themes
from *Wine of the Country* and *Sun In Capricorn* into a unified
conception, much as Faulkner's "big woods" stories, which were
published a few years earlier.

The first of the hunting stories, "The Wild Turkey," is perhaps
the best of them. Written during the war which Hitler's
scapegoating of the Jews precipitated, the story is set on stronger
ground for Basso than a movie-set Bavaria. A hunter himself,
Basso manages the details of the South Carolina turkey hunt with
accurate and imaginative skill. Yet the story is more than a
realistic look at bird-hunting; Basso employs hunting metaphorically to represent the blood fear and the blood knowledge which
violence creates in all men—hunters or not.

The story's two brothers are also would-be warriors. Paul, the
younger at seventeen, has been through basic training in the
marines and will soon be on his way, rather reluctantly, to the
Pacific and the bloody invasions of the Japanese islands. Robert,
the older by a few years, passionately desires a similar mission,
but he cannot leave South Carolina because he has lost a leg in a
hunting accident. The irony of the situation is compounded by
the cause of the accident. Robert, the avid hunter, had forced
Paul, the peaceful farmer, to accompany him on an earlier hunt;
going under a fence Paul left the safety off his shotgun, dropped

the weapon, and shattered Robert's leg. The image of his older brother's horrible wound haunts Paul now on the eve of his initiation into combat.

All the details of the accident came back to him, even to the color of the rusty strands of barbed wire strung between the sagging fence posts, and he could see Robert lying on his back with his face twisted with pain and the bright gush of blood streaming from the wound the blast of the shotgun had made just above the knee, and, protruding from the flesh, the jagged wet splinter of bone which, in a way he had never been able to understand or explain, was part of the bubbling terror of his brother's blood. (27)

On this cold morning Robert has forced his younger brother on another hunt, feeling that Paul must shoot a wild turkey, the most elusive game bird, to prove his manhood before he leaves for the Pacific. Otherwise, Robert feels his peaceful brother will certainly be killed by the proficient Japanese. As they shiver in the turkey blind Robert has built, Paul argues that his older brother should have the first shot. In reality he does not want to kill the gobbler, for he connects the hunt with his brother's awful hurt.

The explosion would be just like the explosion that tore off Robert's leg, and the turkey would die in its own blood, and for an instant, as Paul squinted down the barrels of his gun, he stared into a future which he wished he could escape. He could feel his brother's eyes upon him, commanding him to shoot, and there were a few moments of raging stillness in which his will wrestled with Robert's will, his fear of rousing his brother's anger darkened and confused by all the similar fear he had known in the past. (27)

Finally, Paul refuses to shoot, and the sound of his voice flushes the birds. Robert jumps to fire but misses because of his unsteady balance on his wooden leg. Then he turns in rage on Paul, lifting the butt of the shotgun above his brother's head, a look of hatred twisting his face. Robert rages about his lost leg, his lost chances for glory in the war, the lost triumph of the hunt. Then his voice breaks and he begins to cry in frustrated sorrow. After this catharsis, Paul feels a sudden lightness; his fear has left him, and he is now ready to face his difficult future more securely.

The metaphorical use of the hunt reinforces the Cain-Abel overtones of the final confrontation. Robert, the hunter, the man of violence, is victimized by violence. Paul, the farmer, the man of peace, must also face violence and know it, but when he does he lives. The implications of Basso's conclusion are clear; Paul has found a balance in a violent world while Robert has not. This complex and important theme, realized very completely in the confrontation of the brothers, makes this effort Basso's best and most important story. The skill of the writing, particularly the descriptions of nature, insures its excellence. "The Wild Turkey" proves a story which deserves comparison with the finest of Faulkner's "big woods" pieces.

"King Rail," the last of Basso's stories to be published, in 1947, takes its title from a particularly rare marsh bird, the elusive quarry of many lifelong bird hunters. As in the first of Basso's hunting stories, "The Wild Turkey," bird-hunting is used as a metaphor to describe more universal human activities. As in the earlier story, an older, experienced hunter rages when a younger, more peaceful man refuses to shoot the prize bird. The differences between the two characters represent the wide divergence in human attitudes toward instinctive violence.

The story is notable among Basso's efforts because of its complex double first-person narration. It is introduced by an authorial "I" who explains the situation. He and a friend are hunting duck in the marshes of the Connecticut River with the help of an experienced guide. After a successful day's hunting, the three stop at a local roadhouse to share their stories and a few beers. Soon the guide, Christian Veal, a powerful man of nearly sixty, is relating the story of a king rail he saw the year before. One of his regular rail-hunting clients had brought a quiet young man up to Connecticut with him, insisting that Christian pole his boat while he goes off with a second guide. Although Christian works hard all morning he only finds the young man three shots, and he misses the first two. When he hits the third and Christian recovers the tiny body, the young man is revolted. He has spent the war years in China, and he compares the sport to shooting sparrows from a ricksha. Christian is upset by this remark, but he goes into a rage when a king rail rises nearby and the young man declines to shoot. As he poles the skiff back to the cars Christian feels as if he could almost smash the young man's skull with the pole in his hands. Later the older hunter tries to smooth over the situation, but he only makes Christian angrier when he tells him that the young man had said that the guide reminded him of a "Chinaman."

Like the peaceful younger brother in "The Wild Turkey," this sensitive young man has seen too much violence to enjoy killing small birds. His attitude proves incomprehensible to the older Christian, who is assured of the certainties of the hunt and who has been spared the full horrors of the war. To the young man, this "Christian" American seems at heart a Chinese warlord, the destructive spirit of the swamp. His attitude is an exaggeration, for Christian Veal is basically a sportsman and an honest person in his human dealings. Yet he does get mad enough to throw his powerful body on the slight young man, and he is finally intolerant of other attitudes toward hunting. Christian is a New Englander akin to Robert Frost's "good neighbor" in the poem "Mending Wall"; there is much of the "old-stone savage armed" in Christian, as there is in Robert, the South Carolinian. The hunt pursued too lustily becomes an atavistic rite which unfortunately parallels the violence of the modern world. Basso's story subtly and successfully makes its point as the "I" narrator obviously understands more than Christian, and the careful reader understands more than both of them.

"The Age of Fable" is a story of fishing rather than hunting, and it forms a pair with the later story "The Edge of Wilderness." The stories appeared in 1945 and 1947 issues of the *New Yorker*. Mirroring the difference between the two sports, Basso's fishing stories are quieter and more contemplative; both seem somewhat autobiographical, and both have the ring of experience lovingly ordered in fiction. Like the hunting stories, these two tales of fishing explore the unseen depths of human experience; something almost archetypal appears in the recreation of these traditional human activities for sport.

The age of fable proves to be that level of experience, whether for the individual or the race, when golden dreams of future glories were still possible. For Peter Maxwell, Basso's rather literary protagonist, the age of fable is past. He has just turned forty in the midst of history's most destructive war. He has not lived up to his dreams for himself, nor has he seen humanity live up to its best visions of itself. Now he must face his realities as a limited person in a fallen, limited world.

Maxwell always celebrates his birthday by trout-fishing in the mountains of North Carolina where his father, now dead, had taken him fishing as a child. This year for the first time he takes along his own son, Patrick, who is only six. As they walk the forest path to a pool in the mountains, Maxwell can see himself being helped over the same obstacles by his father. Patrick is doubly excited because Maxwell has promised to introduce him to an Indian who lives close by the stream they intend to fish. When they near the stream Patrick reminds him of his promises; they must visit the Indian and then catch a trout.

Maxwell is both amused and disturbed by the boy's insistence. He is not even sure if the old Indian is still alive or if he can still catch a trout in these played-out waters. He does not want to disappoint his son, who still lives in the age of fable. Because he does still have his visions, the boy is disappointed by the prosaically named Cherokee, Joe.

Maxwell was beginning to think the Indian must be off in the woods somewhere when he came to the door. He looked very old and wrinkled. He wore only a pair of dirty overalls and torn gray felt hat that was streaked with old sweat stains. One corner of the loose bib of the overalls hung down on his chest, revealing the bones of his ribs beneath his mahogany-colored skin, and his arms were thin and wasted. The hound stopped barking when he came to the door. (18)

The boy had been expecting the Plains Indian chief in full regalia who decorated his picturebook at home.

The fishing also disappoints Patrick, and he soon wants to go home. Maxwell feels strangely deserted as he wades into the creek alone, trying to forget the Indian's advice, "Fish no good. . . . Most all gone. Pretty soon no fish left" (18). For a while he works desperately to make a strike, but comes up with nothing. Then, as Maxwell is turning to leave, the granddaddy of all trout explodes from the water to strike his hook. Maxwell skillfully handles the fish, but it breaks the line around a snag and escapes. The father turns, expecting to find the son even more disappointed in him. To his surprise the boy is alive with excitement; he chatters happily on the way back to the Indian's cabin, where he insists on stopping. Then they turn toward home.

The boy ran ahead of Maxwell and scampered up the path. Maxwell felt very grateful to him. It was a strange thing, being grateful to a child, and he could not get used to it. He suspected, however, walking up the path that wound through so much of his life, touching on love and death and early sorrow, that it had something to do with the fact that today was his birthday and that the age of fable was past. (20)

The boy has recreated the age of fable for Maxwell. In the midst of the realities of war, in the inheritance of the complexities of history, wonder can still exist. Maxwell realizes that the individual and the race constantly renew themselves in the little rituals repeated from the past. His lively son recalls both his dead father and his own past self, his own age of fable. Even Cherokee Joe's proud past as hunter and fisherman are recalled in that single strike. The grandfather trout still alive in the played-out pool confirms the reality behind the dream visions of the age of fable. Maxwell has restored Patrick's faith in him, but more importantly Patrick has restored his father's faith in the fabulous.

"The Edge of Wilderness," published in the *New Yorker* for September 20, 1947, continues the fishing experiences of young Patrick Maxwell. Now almost eight, the boy is a proven fisherman; he has caught three brook trout, though the "granddaddy" of the pool has escaped him. His fishing prowess is only one indication of his maturity; in the two years between stories, he has visited Arizona with his parents, learned to ride a horse, and been taught to swear by some cowboys proficient in the art. In fact, his father has had to caution him about using "corral" language in the house, especially in front of his mother.

On the day depicted in the story Patrick is fishing an accessible part of the stream, still in pursuit of the big trout that got away. He is disturbed by an older man wading the stream and casting wildly about with a metal rod. Patrick's curiosity is aroused by the man's unusual outfit; he wears black trousers and a collarless white shirt. When he introduces himself, the stranger explains his outlandish outfit. He is the Reverend Wagstaff of the First Baptist Church of Piney Knoll, Mississippi, visiting his niece in this area. His pants are his special "baptizing" trousers, elegant but waterproofed. He describes his last baptismal as three hours long, with much ducking and dunking, but his pants never let in any water.

Patrick, raised in more liberal religious traditions, does not believe a word of this, and his expression gives his doubt away to the minister. Later, when the minister reveals that he has not

had a nibble all afternoon, Patrick brags about the three trout he
has taken on other days. Irritated at his own lack of success and
the boy's attitude toward baptism, the Reverend Wagstaff
implies that Patrick has told "a whopper." Patrick manages to
hold his temper until the minister leaves, and then he bursts out
in coarsest "corral" language.

"The old grown-up stinker," he said bitterly. "Calling that old pair of
pants baptizing trousers! As if I'd believe that! Saying he dunked
people under the water and held them there! As if I didn't know they
would drown if he did! And he tried to make out that *I* was telling a lie,
the old goddam stinking grown-up bastard!" (75)

The story has considerably more meaning than a short
summary indicates, and this meaning becomes more clear when
it is compared with "The Age of Fable." Patrick obviously still
lives in the age of fable. Thus he is still able to endow events with
fabulous significance, particularly those events which his father
also found important, such as hooking the "granddaddy" trout.
The Reverend Wagstaff's refusal of belief is as much of a shock
to the boy as Patrick's doubts about baptism are to the minister.
As in many of Hemingway's stories the fishing expeditions are
rituals of immersion which parallel the baptismal rituals of the
Christian tradition. The minister's denial of Patrick's ritual
shakes his childish faith in the magical order of things. The
minister parallels Joe, the Cherokee Indian, in the earlier story;
the freckled, fat, red-faced Reverend Wagstaff is not Patrick's
picture of a minister, and his baptizing seems as outlandish as his
fishing outfit. Finally, Patrick will have to come to terms with
this more difficult image, and Basso's story implies that with
maturity he will, much as his father, Peter, has done. Thus, the
two fishing stories develop more positive aspects of the rituals of
the chase than stories which depict the ambiguous violence of
hunting.
    "A Kind of a Special Gift," published in the *New Yorker* for
February 24, 1945, forms a pair with "The Broken Horn," which
appeared later that year, in the October 6 issue of the same
magazine. Both stories are set in a nameless small town
somewhere in Northern Louisiana, a parish seat which seems
much like Montrose, the setting of *Sun In Capricorn* (1942). This
novel was the last done by Basso before the period of the hunting

stories, and it seems natural that he would turn back to a setting recently developed. "The Broken Horn," the story of an obsessive hunt, recalls one of the subplots in *Days Before Lent* (1941), Ned Ravenwill's death struggle with "Old Red." The general ambience of the Southern small town and the amiable older men of the stories remind the reader of Basso portraits in even earlier novels such as *Cinnamon Seed* (1934) and *Courthouse Square* (1936).

"A Kind of a Special Gift" is narrated by an unnamed twelve-year-old boy, a typical Southern youngster interested in hunting and fishing and little else. Like preadolescents in many Southern stories, Robert Penn Warren's "Blackberry Winter," for example, this young man comes to learn something of the difficulty of adult life from the observation of the adult eccentricity around him. The center of attention is his Uncle Zebulon, a childless lawyer of sixty, who is best known as the trainer of the best bird dogs in the region. Not much of a hunter himself, Uncle Zebulon uses his dogs to chase up birds for his best friend, Major Josephus Bedford, the central character in "The Broken Horn."

The old lawyer's special favorite, of all the dogs he ever owned, is an English Setter named Bess. Evidently he named her after the "Good Queen," for he often expostulates on the dog's regal quality.

"Old Bess is like a queen," he would say. "Not just an accident queen, not just somebody who happened to get born to wear a crown, but a proud and lovely lady with a natural queenliness that shows in everything she does or says. It's a pleasure just to watch the way she goes after birds. She always finds them, as all you fellows know. But I don't care whether she finds them or not. It's the way she does it that counts. There's a style and a proudness in just the way she walks. She *knows* she's a queen." (24)

Unfortunately, Uncle Zebulon loses Bess and all his other dogs, save one sorry pointer, to the dumb rabies. The old man is brokenhearted, and overnight he turns "queer," the town's genteel term for crazy.

The nephew often comes upon his uncle striding the hills around the town without a gun or a dog. On one occasion Uncle Zebulon confesses that he is developing his sense of smell, and he claims that his senses are becoming as acute as a good bird dog's.

Such talk in the town barbershop, the unofficial meeting place of the sporting fraternity, leads to a ten-dollar bet. Followed by half the town Uncle Zebulon leads Major Bedford out into the field, sniffing all the way.

My uncle, his head in the air, gave no sign that he had heard. He kept on walking across the pea field, breathing deeply, and suddenly stopped dead still. Major Bedford, who all this time had been walking a few yards behind him, now began to go toward him. My uncle slowly lifted his arm and pointed to a spot in the pea field about twenty feet from where he was standing; it was the most regal gesture I have ever seen. (27)

The silence is broken by the squeal of brakes, and Zebulon's two younger brothers charge through the crowd and half cajole, half drag the old man off to the car. After a family conference Uncle Zebulon visits a doctor in New Orleans and then goes off on a three-month vacation. He comes back seemingly cured of his obsession, for he never mentions his scenting abilities again. Yet, his nephew still wonders about him.

Every now and then, though, he would go walking in the country all by himself, and occasionally, when I was out with Ranger, I would happen to come upon him. He would always be standing very still, rapt and absorbed, and he seemed to be smelling very hard. (27)

Uncle Zebulon's obsession finally proves too curious and too inconsequential for the matter of really fine fiction. Rather, his bizarre behavior is the stuff of poignant comedy, a mode successfully worked by many Southern writers such as Eudora Welty and Truman Capote. Uncle Zebulon does have "a kind of a special gift," but it is so strange that his society must exile him for it or force him to forget it. His nephew learns from his observation of his uncle how eccentric human behavior can be; more importantly he also comes to understand how intolerant society can be of special ways of seeing the world. Uncle Zebulon's way is so funny, however, that the story elicits only a bittersweet feeling of agreement with the boy's observation.

Major Josephus Bedford, Uncle Zebulon's best friend, is the central character of another story narrated by the nameless twelve-year-old nephew, "The Broken Horn." The Major, whose rank actually was a brevet commission from the Spanish War, is the area's leading hunter, and working with Uncle Zebulon's dogs he never fails to take his bag. His success is as much motivated by economy as sportsmanship, for the parsimonious Major stocks his larder with the game he shoots. However, his obsession is not his hunting but his means of transportation, an ancient Buick ready to fall apart into junk metal.

The town is astounded when the Major's wife and daughter finally nag him into buying a new car for the daughter's wedding in another town. His new Buick becomes even more of an obsession for the Major, and he polishes the car several times a day with a soft rag. For almost a year he keeps the car without a scratch; then he nearly totals it when he swerves into a ditch to avoid hitting a huge buck deer. After recovering, the Major finds a piece of the deer's horn on the road and swears vengeance against this particular animal. Through the months of the deer season, he pursues the buck with the broken horn single-mindedly, but with no success.

Uncle Zebulon proves understanding of his friend's obsessive hunt, though the town judges that the Major has also gotten "queer." At the same time, the fame of the buck has spread through the region, and others join in the hunt. None is successful. The animal assumes a near-legendary status; "he became more a creature of fable than a living thing" (30). Of course, this is what the buck has become for the Major; like Uncle Zebulon's bird dog Bess, the buck is part of the age of fable which these old men, entering their second childhood, wish to recapture. The Major's vision is destroyed when a "white-trash" sharecropper shoots the deer from his kitchen window. The Major is brokenhearted and retreats to his farm, almost never hunting again. The story concludes with a visit from Uncle Zebulon and his nephew. The lawyer has brought his old friend a pair of fighting chickens. "I sure hope he gets interested in those chickens," he concludes. "A man without an interest is a sorry thing" (31).

Both Uncle Zebulon and Major Bedford are more comic than tragic as protagonists. The Major's hunt has none of the tragic obsession of Ned Ravenwill's quest of Old Red, for example. Yet their portraits go beyond the sort of colorful eccentricity featured in *New Yorker* sketches over the years. The two childish old men are recreating the age of fable through their hunting, and the narrator nephew, then at the point of adolescence, now in adulthood looking back, understands something about his own youth. Thus these stories compare very nicely with the two fishing stories featuring Peter and Patrick Maxwell; "A Kind of a Special Gift" and "The Broken Horn" are the least serious of the hunting stories, but they still prove to be interesting and rewarding reading.

The unification of the hunting and fishing stories around the thematic ambiguity of these atavistic sports adds a special dimension to these half-dozen pieces; but taken as individual works all of them remain fine short stories. The earlier efforts from the 1930s are less successful, though still interesting to the student of Basso's work. In conclusion, the ten stories Basso wrote cause the critic to wish that the author had turned out a much greater number. The freedom from the restraint of commercially acceptable plotting, the chance to experiment with new themes and techniques, and the use of autobiographical materials make the story an important form for Basso. Unfortunately he did not write enough stories to achieve either a complete mastery of the form or a significant development of new materials for his novels.

CHAPTER 8

Nonfiction Writing

ALTHOUGH this study has emphasized Hamilton Basso's fiction, his most important contribution to American literature, it also has made frequent reference to the author's nonfiction. Fiction was Basso's first love, but until the success of *The View From Pompey's Head*, it was nonfiction that supported his novels. Hamilton Basso was a working journalist through most of his career, progressing from the New Orleans newspapers to the great national magazines published in New York. In addition to the voluminous material produced as a part of his working routine, Basso also published four volumes of nonfiction: the biography, *Beauregard: The Great Creole* (1933); the collection of short biographies, *Mainstream* (1943); the series of travel sketches, *A Quota of Seaweed* (1960); as well as his 1952 edition of William Lewis Herndon's *Exploration of the Valley of the Amazon* (1854). Much of this material proves important as background to Basso's fiction, but much of it is also valuable as fine nonfiction writing. In order to complete the account of Hamilton Basso as a writer, this chapter will present a brief overview of his nonfiction.

Hamilton Basso's nonfiction prose, like his novels and stories, can best be viewed within the literary perspectives established in Chapter 1, the perspectives of the Southern Renaissance and of liberal Realism. Like his fiction, most of Basso's nonfiction concerns the South, and the material proves most important as background for his novels. In its own right, Basso's nonfictional analysis of the South provides a unified view of the region, its strengths, and its problems. It should be remembered that the modern Renaissance in the South extended beyond *belles lettres*. During the same decades that Wolfe, Faulkner, Warren, and Tennessee Williams were revealing the soul of the South in their works, a similar revelation was taking place in the humanities

141

and the social sciences. The Southern myth was reexamined by historians like C. Vann Woodward, sociologists like Howard Odum and Rupert Vance, and critics like Wilbur J. Cash in his classic study, *The Mind of the South* (1941). All of these writers and many others presented a realistic reassessment of the Southern myth from the viewpoint of liberal political ideas. Hamilton Basso's nonfiction forms a part of this reassessment, and it is within this perspective that it proves most valuable.

Of course, Basso's nonfiction, again like his fiction, extended beyond Southern subjects to provide a realistic view of people, places, and events throughout America and the world. As a journalist for national magazines Basso reported on conditions in Europe as well as in other parts of the United States, and later in his career travel writing became one of his major interests. This development can be most easily traced in the three volumes of nonfiction which Basso produced throughout his career. The first, the biography of Beauregard, concerns a Southern, indeed, a New Orleans subject; the second traces "the mainstream" of American life in twelve representative biographies; the third chronicles the author's visits to foreign places as exotic as Honduras and Tahiti. These three books can provide convenient starting points for the discussion of these three general areas of subject matter. The only other important topic in Basso's nonfiction is literature, as he wrote numerous reviews, articles about the state of Southern and American letters, and an important series of *New Yorker* profiles concerned with literary figures. Thus, within a general chronological framework, these four subject areas will structure the discussion of Basso's nonfiction in this chapter.

I   *The South*

Hamilton Basso left Tulane University in 1926 at the age of twenty-two; immediately he began work as a "cub" reporter on the *New Orleans Tribune.* He covered city events without a byline for the *Tribune* and, after his sojourn in New York, for the *New Orleans Item* in 1927. His first nationally published article appeared in 1927; under the title "Flood Water," Basso described the great Mississippi flood of that year for the *New Republic.*[1] The article is presented in a crisp journalistic style with a good feeling for color and detail; it indicates Basso's talent for reportage and also suggests his fictional talent in its colorful descriptions. After trying his hand at several other occupations, including advertising, Basso returned to journalism with the *New Orleans Times-Picayune* in 1929, rising to the position of Night City Editor. During these years Basso also published his first novel, *Relics and Angels* (1929), began his second, and started work on a biography of the Confederate General Beauregard. In order to complete these projects Basso left newspaper work entirely, and settled into full-time writing in a small cabin in the mountains of North Carolina.

Hamilton Basso had always been an acute student of Southern history, and one of his earliest written efforts was a short biography of another New Orleans hero, the Confederate General Mouton, which won a gold medal in a city-wide competition when he was only twelve. Therefore, it was natural that Basso was drawn to the life of the colorful Creole, General P. G. T. Beauregard. Puzzled by the obscurity into which Beauregard's reputation had fallen, Basso discovered that the only biography was, in his words "chocolate coated," and he decided to produce a more realistic portrait. His attitude is made clear in the "Prologue" to the book itself where he attributes the neglect of Beauregard to the preeminence of the Southern myth. His explanations of the myth prefigure Wilbur J. Cash's larger analysis by almost a decade, and like Cash's it identifies the myth with the very mind of the South. The myth produced a picture of the brave Confederate officer, based on Robert E. Lee for the most part, and it rejected any officer who did not fit this mythic mold. Beauregard most definitely did not, and, therefore, the mind of the South effaced his memory.

Born in 1818 at his family's plantation near New Orleans, Beauregard was the oldest son of one of the oldest Creole families. Educated in New York and France, he graduated from West Point in 1838 and was posted to coastal defense work in Louisiana. During the Mexican war he served as an engineer on the staff of General Winfield Scott, receiving two wounds and two brevets for bravery in the attack on Mexico City. Rather piqued because Robert E. Lee and another officer were awarded three brevets, Beauregard impulsively resigned from the army, but was later reinstated. He worked on various engineering projects in Louisiana until 1860 when he was selected as Superintendent of West Point. Arriving in January 1861, he resigned on February 20 and at once accepted an appointment as Brigadier-General in the Confederate Army.

Sent to take charge of the defenses at Charleston, South Carolina, Beauregard led the attack on Fort Sumter which opened the fighting of the Civil War. Now immensely popular, the Creole general was second in command during the Union rout at Bull Run, and he urged the Confederate government to follow up their victory with a drive against Washington. When they rejected his plans Beauregard arrogantly criticized his commanders, earning him a reputation as excitable and unreliable, if brave and chivalrous. In the spring of 1862, he was appointed second in command of all Confederate forces in the western theater with the rank of full general. His commander, General Johnston, was killed at Shiloh, where Beauregard assumed command and fought a skillful retreat against a stronger force. His subsequent withdrawals, though strategically sound, proved very unpopular, and his fame began to decline. In 1863 he was transferred to the defense of Charleston, which he skillfully held for the Confederacy. Later Beauregard out-maneuvered General Butler's army at Drewey's Bluff, helped Lee to defend Petersburg, and retreated across the Carolinas until the surrender at Appomattox.

After the war, the civilian Beauregard served for five years as president of the New Orleans, Jackson, and Mississippi Railway, while declining several offers to serve in foreign armies. In 1870 he became manager of the notorious Louisiana Lottery, and, though it could not be demonstrated that he was personally responsible for any of its chicanery, his reputation was seriously hurt by this association. In spite of the scandalous record of the Lottery, Beauregard also served as Commissioner of Public Works in New Orleans as an Adjutant General of New Orleans until his death in 1893 at the age of seventy-five. His association with the Lottery, his flamboyant image, and the resentment of other ex-Confederate leaders, notably Jefferson Davis, all contributed to his future obscurity—he simply did not fit the mold for Confederate officers cast by Robert E. Lee.

Basso's biography was very well received, with nearly all the reviewers praising its objectivity, its scholarship, and his lively prose. Andrew Lytle, reviewing the book in the *New Republic*, commented: "His [Basso's] writing is easy, at times flawless, and never vague."[2] Several others talked about the book as modern biography, evidently indicating the frequent use of fictional techniques in authorial stance, descriptions, and dialogue. Of course, much of this material would later reappear in Basso's fiction, particularly in the Civil War sequences of *Cinnamon Seed* (1934) and his Civil War novel, *The Light Infantry Ball* (1959). Although Basso's biography has been superseded by later efforts, it remains an informative and interesting work, valuable not merely as background for his fiction, but as excellent nonfiction writing.[3]

Beauregard also indicates Basso's general attitudes toward the South. In his "Prologue," he readily identifies himself as a Southerner, and even admits that like most Southerners he would like to recapture the past, at least the best parts of the past. "We would like to see restored the old feeling of place, a sense of oneness with the land, our old provincialism. We would like to insert into our modern lives the old courtesy, the old warmth and kindness in human relations, something of the rich simplicity of what has come to be known as the good life" (xi). However, he insists on the reality of the worst parts of the Southern past: ". . . a shallow, importunate pride based on material possessions, the dominance of a privileged class maintained by the exploitation of human beings, the exclusion of thousands of plain folk even from labor, and a conviction of racial supremacy based not only on the accident of birth, but also upon the accident of locale" (x–xi). Like Wilbur J. Cash and the other liberal observers of the Southern scene, Basso would insist on this realistic refutation of the Southern myth from *Beauregard* to his ultimate condemnation of Southern Shintoism in *The View From Pompey's Head* (1954).

Cinnamon Seed, published in 1934, confirmed in fiction the portrait of the South delineated in *Beauregard*, and beginning in these years Basso, now an associate editor of the *New Republic*, filled in the details of his picture with his nonfiction. During the 1930s Basso's articles about the South fell into three main groups: analyses of Southern politics, particularly of Louisiana politics and Huey Long; accounts of strikes and trials which symbolized the social turbulence of the period in the South; and discussion of the state of Southern letters. In all of these areas, Basso's analysis affirms his realistic and liberal assessment of the Southern scene. For him the politics of the South indicate the basic belief in the "man on horseback" and the "good old boy";

Huey Long, and to a lesser extent Gene Talmadge and other Southern demagogues, were the logical developments of these beliefs. The racial and labor troubles which exploded at the Scottsboro trial or the Gastonia strike, Basso characterized as products of the South's refusal to think clearly and realistically about the blacks or the working class. Finally, for Basso, Southern literature was divided between apologists for the old order and realists who dramatized the South as it really existed.

Huey Long as a symbol of Southern political life provides the most frequent subject for Basso's articles during the 1930s. With considerable candor, Basso later admitted that like many Louisianans he admired Long as a welcome antidote for the moribund and corrupted political machines created first by the Bourbon old guard and then by the New Orleans gang.[4] However, like other liberals he soon detected Long's crypto-Fascist leanings, and turned absolutely against him. He reviewed Long's campaign autobiography as a work of fiction,[5] compared Long with Hitler,[6] and even after Long's assassination called him an abject failure.[7] Overall, Basso was one of Long's most implacable foes, perhaps because for him Long represented everything wrong with Southern politics. As indicated in Chapter 4, Long received fictional treatment from Basso in *Cinnamon Seed* (1934) and *Sun in Capricorn* (1942), but both fictional portraits of Long are marred by Basso's absolutely negative image of the man as symbol of everything vile in Southern life.

Other major problems of Southern life, the labor and racial questions, received analysis in Basso's reports on Southern strikes, lynching, and trials. Aside from the textile strike at Gastonia, North Carolina, in 1934, one of the major labor confrontations of the decade, Basso also covered the strikes at Augusta and Macon, Georgia, as well as at Tarreytown, South Carolina.[8] Basso's sympathies are entirely with the strikers, victims of exploitation because the Southerner still believed in the possibility of genteel paternalism. As Wilbur J. Cash also pointed out, the mill owner, even if an absentee Yankee, inherited the traditional respect accorded the plantation owner; thus strikers were viewed as rebellious servants, as dangerous as "uppity" blacks. Basso acutely analyzed this sort of defensive racial attitude as the cause of lynchings and "kangaroo court" trials such as the infamous Scottsboro case. Basso's report

remains one of the best accounts of this celebrated trial because
he combines this basically accurate analysis with the insights of
fictional methodology.[9] Again this material finds its way into
Basso's novels: *In Their Own Image* (1935) recreates the textile
strikes, while *Courthouse Square* (1936) and *The View From
Pompey's Head* (1954) involve trials much like the Scottsboro
case.

Basso's several analyses of Southern literature and his many
reviews of Southern books also illustrate his overall positions on
the Southern mind. In 1935 he divided the writers of the
Southern Renaissance into two dichotomized groups; on the one
side the defenders of the tradition, mainly the Nashville
Agrarians; on the other side, the realistic attackers of the
tradition, including himself, Faulkner, Wolfe, Erskine Caldwell,
T. S. Stribling, and any other writers he liked.[10] His assessments
of individual writers and works were then decided by which
camp the writer represented; for example, he found T. S.
Stibling more important than several of the Agrarians.[11] More
recent criticism would find fault with Basso's categorizations and
evaluations, but his conclusions were echoed by others in his
time (Wilbur J. Cash, for example), and they are the logical
extension of his social attitudes. Basso's views of Southern writers
will also be considered below in a general discussion of his views
on literature.

II *America*

When Basso became an associate editor of the *New Republic*,
his reportage naturally extended beyond the South. From his
editorial base in New York, Basso covered national politics, labor
and racial conflicts, and literature. Although his well-developed
views on the mind of the South were not as apparent in these
pieces, his liberal and realistic attitudes were extended to
national questions. Like most American liberals Basso was an
enthusiastic supporter of President Franklin D. Roosevelt and
the New Deal, and several of his essays affirm this support.[12]
Basso also pilloried demagogues outside of the South, such as
Maury Maverick of Texas, Father Coughlin, the radio priest, and
most notably the newspaper czar William Randolph Hearst.[13] His
account of a race riot in Harlem connected national problems
with Southern attitudes, and national strikes were viewed in the

same frame of reference as Southern labor troubles.[14] Finally, aside from placing Southern writers, like Wolfe and Faulkner, in national contexts Basso also reviewed non-Southern books and commented on the national literary scene.

Basso's major assessment of the national character was *Mainstream*, published in 1943, an attempt to trace the main currents of national life through the capsule biographies of a dozen representative Americans. (Interestingly, four of his twelve are Southerners, necessitating considerable discussions of the South.) After opening with the assertion of a general American character, in spite of all its multifarious variations, Basso attempts to chart its development like the course of a river system, mapping "the larger tributaries in whose mergings we see the mainstream of tradition" (xi). Beginning with the familiar pairing of Puritan and Cavalier, Basso presents Cotton Mather and John Smith, contrasting their basic influence on the American mind. Next he contrasts Thomas Jefferson as American Democrat and John Calhoun as American Aristocrat; this contrastive pairing continues with two kinds of American success story, Abraham Lincoln's and Andrew Carnegie's. All of these choices are conventional enough, particularly in Basso's preference for Smith, Jefferson, and Lincoln. A more daring combination is P. T. Barnum and Henry Adams as educators of the American mind on a popular and scholarly level. Basso then groups four politicians into two contrasting pairs: William Jennings Bryan and Theodore Roosevelt; Huey Long and Franklin D. Roosevelt. If Long's inclusion seems startling, Basso insists that the American has always been something of a demagogue, an inevitable foil for the democrat. Finally, he finishes as he began, with a composite portrait of John Applegate, an average American. (This "average American" was a favorite type in the popular culture of the period, particularly in Frank Capra's movies such as *Meet John Doe*, which appeared in 1941).

Bassos' book was generally well received; it was positively reviewed by critics like August Derleth, Albert Guerard, Merle Curti, and Jonathan Daniels, and it sold well in that war year when public attention was turned to more immediate matters concerning American life. The negative criticism the book elicited was posited in terms of Basso's choices (particularly of Huey Long) or in terms of John Applegate's inherent Babbittry.

Perhaps the strain of the war years caused Basso to stress the optimism of the American Dream, but this quality seems, as in Capra's movies, rather dated and naive. All the same, the book still proves readable and interesting, perhaps most in its prefiguration of more scholarly work in the developing discipline of American Studies. *Mainstream* is a book which should be more often remembered. It is also interesting to note that Basso's probing of the American character was paralleled in his fiction. His next novel published after *Mainstream, The Greenroom* (1949) concerns an American, symbolically a Westerner from Arizona, in the Jamesian situation of unraveling a complex human problem in a foreign setting, in this case, France.

III *The World*

Although Hamilton Basso continued to write about the South and America, the French setting of *The Greenroom* represents the increasing tendency of his nonfiction to consider world subjects. Basso had made his first trip to Europe in 1938, and even earlier his stories and articles had considered the rise of Fascism.[15] After World War II, Basso turned to writing travel articles, as background for his fiction as well as a source of income. His first efforts described familiar landscapes, Louisiana, New Orleans, and Savannah, Georgia; the last article also was the inspiration for the Pompey's Head novels. Later he considered other American settings: Los Angeles, St. Louis, San Francisco, and Wyoming. Basso proved a fine travel writer, with a novelist's sense of place and people, so naturally his talents were extended to foreign scenes: Jamaica, Havana, Rio de Janeiro, Spain, Honduras, Samoa, Tahiti, and Scandinavia. Most of these travel pieces appeared either in the *New Yorker*, where Basso worked from 1944 to 1961, or in *Holiday* magazine.

In 1952 Basso edited a new edition of William Lewis Herndon's *Exploration of the Valley of the Amazon*, a valuable description of South America first published in 1854. Herndon was an American naval officer commissioned by Congress to explore the Amazon to its headwaters, which he did in 1851. His account, printed as a government document, interested the American public, in particular the young Samuel Clemens, in South America. Basso rediscovered the book during his reading for his own trip to Brazil, reedited it (excising factual data only of interest to Herndon's commissioners), and provided a nicely written introduction. The book was widely praised, except for a few academic critics who quibbled with Basso's excisions or his placement of Herndon's book within the exploration literature of South America.

His last work of nonfiction, *A Quota of Seaweed* (1960), brought together the best of his foreign travel sketches from the *New Yorker* and *Holiday*. Basso unified the volume by stressing those places which still preserved a primitive vitality outside the direct influences of modern commercial civilization. He followed Herndon's path up the Amazon in Brazil, visited remote villages in the Spanish *montana*, explored the sleazy ports of Honduras, sojourned in Jamaica, and finally tried to recover the vision of Robert Louis Stevenson and Paul Gaugin in Tahiti and Samoa. Like his other nonfiction works, this one was also very positively reviewed. Only one reviewer, Third World novelist V. S. Naipaul, complained about the book, accurately observing that Basso decried the coming of the American tourist to each of his primitive places while acting rather like a stereotyped tourist himself. Aside from this real flaw, the sketches are colorful and lively, not pieces for a travel guide but gatherings of interesting data about the places described.

IV *Literature*

A similar opening out of Basso's vision from Southern to American to world perspectives can be used to structure a discussion of the writer's pieces on literature. At the outset it should be made clear that Basso was no literary theorist, and he rarely commented on his own works. Rather his literary essays fall into three types, all journalistic genres; the review, the profile, and the reminiscence. Basso was a prolific reviewer of all sorts of books, volumes on everything from philosophy to Broadway. His most important reviews concern works close to his own, and these have been listed in the Bibliography below These reviews of Southern novels generally follow the pattern of his overall vision of Southern letters outlined earlier; those in his camp he approved of, those in the enemy camp he disparaged. The same pattern is evident in reviews of books in American and world literature; Basso likes the writers he feels are liberal realists like himself: Fitzgerald and Hemingway, Somerset Maugham and Thomas Mann.

In the years that Basso worked for the *New Yorker* he wrote a number of their well-known "profiles," some on literary subjects, but others on painters, philosophers, cartoonists, actors, and such. His best-known literary profile was of Eugene O'Neill, America's greatest dramatist. Basso, already an acquaintance of O'Neill's, had several long conversations with the playwright in the autumn of 1947, a period when O'Neill was suffering from artistic as well as personal problems. To Basso, "O'Neill, at the present time, could be a figure waiting in the wings for a cue in a play by Eugene O'Neill—the tragic life thrice compounded."[16] His profile, entitled "Tragic Sense," appeared in the *New Yorker* on February 28, March 6, and March 13, 1948, and it is still considered an important assessment of O'Neill's career, as well as a valuable source of biographical information.

In the same year that the profile of O'Neill was published Basso proposed a similar piece on his old friend William Faulkner. The very private Faulkner declined the honor, but invited Basso to drop by for a drink anytime he was in Oxford, Mississippi. Basso's vision of Faulkner was delayed until the Mississippian's death in 1962, when his friend wrote the well-known reminiscence published in the *Saturday Review*.[17] Much like an earlier reminiscence of another friend, Thomas Wolfe, Basso's article combines a judicious literary assessment with a number of warm personal memories.[18] Like the O'Neill profile, both of these reminiscence pieces are cited by the biographers of their subjects as important sources.[19]   As a working journalist and a person of wide-ranging interest Basso wrote nonfiction on many subjects—from Roman Catholicism to baseball—not included in the categories outlined above, but this work was for the most part occasional and ephemeral. The important subjects of Basso's nonfiction were literature, travel, the American scene, and the South. All of these subjects were treated with a liberal Realism rooted in the reality of the Southern Renaissance. Because of this orientation Basso's nonfiction works are historically valuable as examples of the traditions which inform them; however, beyond this value they provide considerable insights into Basso's fiction, and they often prove to be interesting and enjoyable prose works in their own right.

CHAPTER 9

Some Conclusions

F ROM the outset this study has emphasized Basso's place as a writer of the Southern Renaissance, one of the most important movements in American literary history. Both his biography and his bibliography emphasize this placement. Basso was born and grew up in the South; he lived most of his adult life in the South, and even when he settled permanently in the Connecticut suburbs of New York City, he still remained the Southerner *deraciné*, the Southerner trying to go home again in his books. The greatest part of his voluminous output in both fiction and nonfiction was directly concerned with the South, with Southern settings, characters, and themes. Almost all of his newspaper work, the most important part of his magazine journalism, and nine of his eleven novels demonstrate his continuing interest in the South.

Basso wrote widely and well about Southern problems and Southern people; although he cannot be counted in the first rank of Southern writers, he provides an interesting and incisive picture of the South from the Depression to the Supreme Court Decision on desegregation. Both his fiction and his nonfiction were widely read and readily accepted, particularly by Northern liberal audiences; thus Basso may have done as much as almost any single figure in shaping modern American attitudes toward the South. This seems particularly true in terms of his carefully considered liberal Realism, which marked his work from 1929 to 1964. Over these thirty-five years, almost a generation, Basso courageously presented and defended his essential viewpoint in spite of shifting intellectual and literary fashions.

But Basso is an important writer in more than a sociological sense. He may be the finest realistic novelist produced by the Southern Renaissance. Even more importantly he is simply a fine fictionist. Novels such as *Cinnamon Seed, Courthouse Square,*

Days Before Lent, The Greenroom, and *The View From Pompey's Head* and his fine stories of hunting and fishing should have more than an historical interest for a contemporary audience. They are all eminently readable, intelligent, and often exciting fiction. Basso consistently created novels which dealt complexly with the most difficult topical problems and current ideas. His themes are most often realistic and intellectual in the best senses of those two often misused words. His ideas anticipated by decades concerns which have become universally important today, such as ecology, structural anthropology, and preventive medicine.

Basso also embodied these ideas and themes in well-drawn characters, particularly his autobiographical protagonists; in well-told narratives; and in always-readable prose. Even his weakest novels give the reader the pleasure of a smooth-reading and smooth-moving story. When this story involved the complex maturation process of one of his intellectual heroes, Dekker Blackheath of *Cinnamon Seed,* David Barondess of *Courthouse Square,* or Anson Page of *The View from Pompey's Head,* Basso often created genuinely first-rate fiction. He also peopled his books with a gallery of colorful minor characters from crusty old maiden aunts to tobacco-spitting, "good old boy" sheriffs and hunters. His stories, whether of plagues in the Louisiana Bayou or of Jamesian intrigues in a French *château,* nearly always hold his readers' attention. In novels such as *Days Before Lent* or *The Greenroom,* where he has all of these elements working well together, his fiction deserves comparison with the best produced by the Southern Renaissance.

It must be admitted, as the analyses of individual novels have shown, that Basso does not always get his books together. His characterization, particularly of younger women and of his protagonists' lovers and wives, is sometimes weak. Likewise, his inability to draw fully developed black characters becomes an obvious weakness for a Southern novelist. Often these failures of characterization occur because of a tendency to use his people too symbolically, to typecast them. This problem also becomes obvious in the stock happy endings which often mar his books. Form was always a problem for Basso; though he always plotted very carefully, the overall shape of his novels often provided real difficulties. Novels such as *Relics and Angels, Sun In Capricorn,* and *The Light Infantry Ball,* though basically interesting, display serious difficulties in form. This situation especially obtained in his novels which seem written simultaneously to be vehicles of advanced ideas and objects of commercial literary success; form sometimes did not fit his themes. By the end of his career Basso's smooth, readable style of narration often slid into mere facility. These and other problems combine to weaken books such as *In Their Own Image, Wine of the Country,* and *A Touch of the Dragon.*

Yet for all his very real failures, Basso produced more successful fiction than many writers awarded higher places in the critical pantheon of the Southern Renaissance. Some of the Gothicists command attention out of all proportion to their literary importance in comparison to a popular, realistic, intelligent writer like Hamilton Basso. The continued reevaluation of Southern as well as modern American literature will no doubt adjust some of the imbalances of critical reputation which still exist today. Basso's novels deserve rereading, and they repay careful critical consideration. The present study is intended to encourage this rereading and extend this reconsideration.

Notes and References

Chapter One

1. Stanley J. Kunitz and Howard Haycraft, *Twentieth Century Authors* (New York, 1942), p. 84.

2. *Ibid.*

3. Letter to the author, October 3, 1975, from Mrs. Etolia Basso.

4. Basso's first publication, a poem entitled "Brain," appeared in *The Double Dealer* VII (April, 1925), 139.

5. Mrs. Etolia Basso, *loc. cit.*

6. Joseph Blotner, *Faulkner: A Biography* (New York, 1974), p. 418. 1974), p. 418

7. "William Faulkner, Man and Writer," *Saturday Review of Literature* XLV (July 28, 1962), 411.

8. "Hamilton Basso," *Wilson Library Bulletin* XIV (October 1939), 186.

9. Blotner, *op. cit.*, p. 587

10. LX (October 23, 1929), 274.

11. Mrs. Etolia Basso, *loc. cit.*

12. "Hamilton Basso," *Wilson Library Bulletin* XIV (October 1939), 186.

13. Kunitz and Haycraft, *op. cit.*, p. 85.

14. Mrs. Etolia Basso, *loc. cit.*

15. *Ibid.*

16. Quoted in Daniel Aaron, *Writers on the Left* (New York, 1961), p. 353.

17. "Hamilton Basso," *Wilson Library Bulletin* XIV (October 1939), 186.

18. Mrs. Etolia Basso, *loc. cit.*

19. "Basso Wins Southern Authors Award," *Publishers' Weekly* (February 3, 1940), 625.

20. Mrs. Etolia Basso, *loc. cit.*

21. *Ibid.*

22. *Ibid.*

23. *Ibid.*

24. *New York Herald Tribune Book Review*, October 24, 1954, p. 3.

25. According to Stephen Birmingham in *The Late John Marquand* (New York, 1972), the older writer remarked after reading Basso's

novel ". . . that it seemed more than a case of Basso's having been influenced by *Point of No Return*. It was more like stealing" (p. 213).

26. "Obituary," *New York Times*, May 14, 1964.

27. Mrs. Etolia Basso, *loc. cit.*

28. *Ibid.*

29. Blotner, *op. cit.*, p. 1661.

30. Letter to the author, October 28, 1975, from Mrs. Etolia Basso.

31. "The Writer as Craftsman: The Literary Heroism of Hamilton Basso," *Saturday Review* XLVII (June 27, 1964), 17-18.

32. In *The Burden of Southern History* (Baton Rouge, 1968).

33. F. Garvin Davenport, Jr., *The Myth of Southern History* (Nashville, 1970).

34. New York, 1941.

35. LXXXIII (June 19, 1935), 161-63.

36. "William Faulkner: Man and Writer," 13.

37. See John Bradbury, *Renaissance in the South* (Chapel Hill, 1963).

38. "Realism: An Essay in Definition," *Modern Language Quarterly* X (June, 1949), 184-97.

39. Carbondale, Illinois, 1967.

40. Charlottesville, Virginia, 1969.

41. Quoted in "Hamilton Basso," *American Novelists of Today*, ed. Harry R. Warfel (New York, 1951), p. 26.

Chapter Two

1. Kunitz and Haycraft, *op. cit.*, p. 85.

2. James Rocks, "The World View from Pompey's Head," *South Atlantic Quarterly* LXXI (1972), 333.

3. *New York Herald Tribune Books*, September 8, 1929, p. 19.

4. LX (October 23, 1929), 274.

Chapter Three

1. "The World View from Pompey's Head," 333.

2. *Books*, 8.

Chapter Four

1. *Book Review*, August 6, 1939, p. 5.

2. New York, 1946.

3. "Huey Long Legend" *Life* XXI (December 9, 1946), 106ff.

4. *Ibid.*, 121.

5. See Louis Rubin, Jr., "All the King's Meanings," *Georgia Review* VIII (1954), 422-34.

6. XXV (September 19, 1942), 16.

Chapter Five

1. *Oxford English Dictionary,* "greenroom."
2. Basso's borrowings from *The Great Gatsby* for *Sun In Capricorn* reinforce this view.

Chapter Six

1. *New York Times Book Review,* October 24, 1954, p. 22. (interview by Lewis Nichols).
2. Letter to the author, October 3, 1975, from Mrs. Etolia Basso.
3. "Savannah and the Golden Isles," X (December 1951), 44-57.
4. Interview by Lewis Nichols, *op. cit.*
5. *Book Review,* October 24, 1954, p. 7.
6. E. W. Foell, *Christian Science Monitor,* June 4, 1959, p. 7.
7. *Ibid.*

Chapter Seven

1. The stories are listed in chronological order in the Selected Bibliography; all page references can be checked against these citations.

Chapter Eight

1. LI (June 22, 1927), 123-24.
2. LXXV (May 31, 1933), 79.
3. T. Harry Williams, also the biographer of Huey Long, published the definitive life of Beauregard in Louisiana State University's Southern Biography Series in 1955.
4. "Huey Long Legend," *Life* XXI (December 9, 1946), 106.
5. *New Republic* LXXVIII (February 21, 1934), 54.
6. *Harper's* CLXX (May 1935), 663.
7. *New Republic* C (December 18, 1935), 77.
8. See Bibliography, Part 5, below, where the strike articles are described by the geographical location.
9. "Five Days in Decatur," *New Republic* LXXVII (December 20, 1933) 161-64.
10. "Letters in the South," *New Republic* LXXXIII (June 19, 1935), 161-63.
11. *New Republic* LXXIX (June 20, 1934), 161.
12. "Pulse of the Nation," *New Republic* LXXXIV (August 21, 1935), 41-43; "Hats in the Ring," *New Republic* CII (February 12, 1940), 201-203; "That Man in the White House," *New Republic* CIII (July 22,

1940), 106-108; and "Roosevelt's Legend," *Life* XXIII (November 3, 1947), 126-28.

13. "Maury Maverick: A Portrait," *New Republic* XC (April 21, 1937), 315-17; "Radio Priest in Person," *New Republic* LXXXIII (June 4, 1935), 96-98; "Mr. Hearst Sees Red," *New Republic* LXXXI (January 16, 1935) 269-71; and "Mr. Hearst's Apostolic Creed," *New Republic* LXXII (May 8, 1935), 358-61.

14. "Riot in Harlem," *New Republic* LXXXII (April 3, 1935), 209-10.

15. "Fabulous Man," *Scribners Monthly* XCVII (April 1935), 217-18; "Italian Notebook: 1938," *New Republic* XCV (June 15, 1938), 147-49.

16. Quoted from Basso's working notes in Louis Schaeffer's *O'Neill: Son and Artist* (Boston, 1973), p. 601; Schaeffer attests to the importance of Basso's profile.

17. "William Faulkner: Man and Writer" (June 28, 1962), 11-14.

18. "Thomas Wolfe: A Summing Up," *New Republic* CIII (September 23, 1940), 422-23.

19. See Andrew Turnbull's *Thomas Wolfe* (New York, 1967) and Joseph Blotner's *Faulkner: A Biography* (New York, 1974).

Selected Bibliography

The following bibliography lists all of Hamilton Basso's book-length publications, including the one work which he edited. These are divided into novels, and nonfiction books. The listing of stories and poems is also complete. The nonfiction section is selective, however, listing only those pieces which have important statements about literature, fiction, the South, or Basso's own background. (Basso wrote hundreds of journalistic pieces, and it would be impossible to list them all.) Academic criticism on Basso has been sparse, but many fine comments can be found in reviews of individual novels, which can be easily located in *Book Review Digest*.

Basso's manuscripts and correspondence were willed to the American Collection at the Beinecke Library of Yale University.

PRIMARY SOURCES

1. Novels

Relics and Angels. New York: Macauley, 1929.
Cinnamon Seed. New York: Scribner, 1934.
In Their Own Image. New York: Scribner, 1935.
Courthouse Square. New York: Scribner, 1936.
Days Before Lent. New York: Scribner, 1939.
Wine of the Country. New York: Scribner, 1941.
Sun In Capricorn. New York: Scribner, 1942.
The Greenroom. Garden City: Doubleday, 1949.
The View From Pompey's Head. Garden City: Doubleday, 1954.
The Light Infantry Ball. Garden City: Doubleday, 1959.
A Touch of the Dragon. New York: Viking, 1964.

2. Nonfiction Books

Beauregard, The Great Creole (biography). New York: Scribner, 1933.
Mainstream (biographical essays). New York: Reynal & Hitchcock, 1943.
(Ed.). William Lewis Herndon, *Exploration of the Valley of the Amazon* (1854). New York: McGraw, 1952.
A Quota of Seaweed (travel essays). Garden City: Doubleday, 1960.

3. Short Stories

"I Can't Dance," *transition* (June 1929) XVI: 127–32.
"Rain on Aspidistra," *transition* (February 1933) XXII: 11–15.
"Fabulous Man," *Scribner's Magazine* (April 1935) XCVII: 217–18.
"Me and the Babe," *New Republic* (April 24, 1935) LXXXII: 308–10.
"The Wild Turkey," *New Yorker* (March 18, 1944) XX: 25–27
"A Kind of a Special Gift," *New Yorker* (February 24, 1945) XX: 24–27
"The Age of Fable," *New Yorker* (June 30, 1945) XXI: 17–20.
"The Broken Horn," *New Yorker* (October 6, 1945) XXI: 28–31.
"The Edge of Wilderness," *New Yorker* (September 20, 1947) XXIII: 71–75.
"King Rail," *New Yorker* (October 18, 1947) XXIII: 105–108.

4. Poems

"Brain," *Double Dealer* (April 1925) VII: 139.
"Questioning," *Double Dealer* (May 1926) VIII: 339.

5. Other Short Pieces

"Flood Water," *New Republic* (June 22, 1927) LI: 123–24. About the Great Mississippi Flood of 1927.
"Letter," *transition* (February 1929 XV: 149–50. Describes literary life in New Orleans.
"Five Days in Decatur," *New Republic* (December 20, 1933) LXXVII: 161–64. "Scottsboro Boys" trial.
"About the Berry Schools," *New Republic* (April 4, 1934) LXXVII: 206–208. About Georgia "Company" schools.
"Divided Southern Front," *New Republic* (May 9, 1934) LXXVII: 360–62. Tarreytown, South Carolina, textile strike.
"Mr. Senator Come Clean," *New Republic* (February 21, 1934) LXXVIII: 54. Review of Huey Long's autobiography.
"The End of a Trilogy," *New Republic* (June 20, 1934) LXXIX: 161. Review of T. S. Stribling's *Unfinished Cathedral*.
"Gastonia: Before the Battle," *New Republic* (September 19, 1934) LXXX: 148–49. Major textile strike.
"Two Sides of the Barricades," *New Republic* (October 10, 1934) LXXX: 238–39. Augusta, Georgia, textile strike.
"Strike-buster: Man Among Men," *New Republic* (December 12, 1934) LXXXI: 124–26. Macon, Georgia, textile strike.
"Let's Look at the Record," *New Republic* (February 20, 1935) LXXXII: 41–42. Contains Huey Long material.

"Huey Long and His Background," *Harper's* (May 1935) CLXX: 663-73. Huey Long as a little Hitler.

"Letters in the South," *New Republic* (June 19,1935) LXXXIII: 161-63. Important essay on Modern Southern literature.

"The Kingfish: In Memoriam," *New Republic* (December 18, 1935) C: 177 ". . . He could have been the foremost American democrat."

"Death and Legacy of Huey Long," *New Republic* (January 1, 1936) LXXXV: 215-18.

"Our Gene," *New Republic* (February 19, 1936) LXXXVI: 35-37. Another Southern demagogue.

"Thomas Wolfe: A Portrait," *New Republic* (June 24, 1936) LXXXVII: 199-202. An affectionate portrait.

"Cardinal Pacelli and Father John," *New Republic* (October 28, 1936) LXXXVIII: 343-45. Father John of *Days Before Lent* had a real model.

"Thomas Mann and a New Humanism," *New Republic* (March 9, 1938) XCIV: 120-23.

"South Wind," *New Republic* (June 1, 1938) XCV: 97-98. About Southern politics.

"Italian Notebook: 1938," *New Republic* (June 15, 1938) XCV: 147-49. Fascism in Italy, 1938.

"Huey's Louisiana Heritage," *New Republic* (August 30, 1939) C: 99-100. The corrupt heritage of Long in Louisiana.

"Future of the South," *New Republic* (November 8, 1939) CI: 70-72. Discusses Southern literature.

"Fate of H. G. Wells," *New Republic* (December 13, 1939) CI: 234-35.

"Can New Orleans Come Back?" *Forum* (March 1940) CIII: 124-28. Discusses aftermath of Huey Long.

"Thomas Wolfe: A Summing Up," *New Republic* (September 23, 1940) CIII: 422-23.

"Tonio Kröger in Egyptian Dress," *New Yorker* (July 22, 1944) XX: 53-54. Review of Thomas Mann's *Joseph*.

"Very Old Party," *New Yorker* (December 30, 1944) XX: 24-28; (January 6, 1945) XXVIII: 32. Profile of Somerset Maugham.

"Huey Long Legend," *Life* (December 9, 1946) XXI: 106-108. Discusses novels based on Long's career.

"Tragic Sense," *New Yorker* (February 28, 1948) XXIV: 34-38 (March 6) 34-38; (March 13, 1948), 37-40. O'Neill profile.

"Bayou Country," *Holiday* (October 1949) VI: 52-63. Travel piece on Louisiana.

"Boswell Detective Story," *Life* (December 4, 1950) XXIX: 93-94.

"Savannah and Golden Isles," *Holiday* (December 1951) X: 44-57. Background for *The View From Pompey's Head*.

"New Orleans Childhood," *New Yorker* (October 9, 1954) XXX: 98-99.
Reminiscence.
"Talkative Windfall," *New Yorker* (December 4, 1954) XXX: 163-64.
Reminiscence of pet parrot.
"Thanks to St. Jude," *New Yorker* (May 7, 1955) XXXI: 92ff.
Reminiscence of New Orleans background.
"William Faulkner, Man and Writer," *SRL* (July 28, 1962) VL: 11-14.
Famous obituary piece.

SECONDARY SOURCES

AARON, DANIEL. *Writers on the Left.* New York, 1961, pp. 352-53. Basso
is briefly mentioned in connection with Malcolm Cowley.
BRADBURY, JOHN. *Renaissance in the South.* Chapel Hill, 1963, pp.
161-62. Gives Basso a high evaluation as a social novelist of the
South.
CAROLAN, PAMELA JEAN. *An Examination of Structure in Hamilton
Basso's "The Greenroom".* Unpublished M.A. Thesis, University of
North Carolina, 1971. Sees Mrs. Porter as the center of the novel.
COWLEY, MALCOLM. "The Writer as Craftsman: The Literary Heroism
of Hamilton Basso," *Saturday Review* (June 27, 1964) XLVII:
17-18. This is a very favorable estimation of Basso by an old friend.
GREEN, ROSE BASILE. *The Italian-American Novel.* Rutherford, New
Jersey, 1973, pp. 117-27. Attempts to view Basso as an Italian-
American writer.
HOFFMAN, FREDERICK J. *Art of Southern Fiction.* Carbondale, Illinois,
1963, p. 25. Dismisses Basso as a popularizing novelist.
IKERD, CLARENCE F. *Hamilton Basso: A Critical Portrait.* Unpublished
Ph.D. Dissertation, University of North Carolina, 1974. Provides a
thorough and intelligent discussion of Basso's life and work.
ROCKS, JAMES. "The World View from Pompey's Head." *South Atlantic
Quarterly* (1972), LXXI: 326-41. Provides the most thorough and
judicious analysis of Basso's work, putting stress on the writer's
place in the Southern Renaissance.
RUBIN, LOUIS D., JR. "All the King's Meanings," *Georgia Review* (1954)
VIII: 422-34. Gives a negative judgment of *Sun In Capricorn* in
comparison with *All the King's Men.*
SNYDER, ROBERT E. "The Concept of Demagoguery: Huey Long and His
Critics," *Louisiana Studies* (1976) XV: 61-84. Concentrates on *Sun
In Capricorn* as a political novel.

Index

163